D0179745

SPIRITUAL MENTORING

A GUIDE for SEEKING and GIVING DIRECTION

Keith R. Anderson
& Randy D. Reese

Foreword by James M. Houston

IVP Books

An imprint of InterVarsity Press
Downers Grove, Illinois

InterVarsity Press
P.O. Box 1400, Downers Grove, IL 60515-1426
World Wide Web: www.ivpress.com
E-mail: email@ivpress.com

InterVarsity Press® is the book-publishing division of InterVarsity Christian Fellowship/USA®, a student movement active on campus at hundreds of universities, colleges and schools of nursing in the United States of America, and a member movement of the International Fellowship of Evangelical Students. For information about local and regional activities, write Public Relations Dept., InterVarsity Christian Fellowship/USA, 6400 Schroeder Rd., P.O. Box 7895, Madison, WI 53707-7895, or visit the IVCF website at <www.intervarsity.org>.

Cover photograph: SuperStock

ISBN 978-0-8308-2210-2

Printed in the United States of America ∞

Library of Congress Cataloging-in-Publication Data

Anderson, Keith, 1949–
    Spiritual mentoring : a guide for seeking and giving direction /
    Keith R. Anderson and Randy D. Reese.
        p.   cm.
    ISBN 0-8308-2210-0 (pbk. : alk. paper)
    1. Spiritual direction.   I. Reese, Randy.   II. Title.
BV5053.A53   1999
253.5'3—dc21   99-21817
                                                                             CIP

P   29   28   27   26   25   24   23   22   21   20   19   18   17   16   15   14   13   12   11
Y   24   23   22   21   20   19   18   17   16   15   14   13   12   11   10   09   08   07

With gratitude always to my mother,
Bertha Marion Liljedahl Anderson,
my first mentor and my best
                              —Keith

To Susan, my partner for the journey,
proof that God shed his grace on me
                              —Randy

Foreword

We are living in a period of disenchantment with "knowledge for knowledge's sake." Certainly in theology we desire that knowledge should be for God's sake, or indeed to help us become more godly. This work, by two experienced pastoral teachers, establishes the nature and practice of spiritual mentoring on a sound theological basis. For Jesus Christ is the mentor par excellence. His life and his words are one—transformative indeed!

Rightly it is observed that the basis of New Testament teaching is the requirement of a "heart relationship" that is much more than mere information. We must have an open heart before God. This then opens us to infinite desires that only God can satisfy, as Augustine describes to us in his *Confessions*. Yet we also join in the communion of saints, a companionship through rich historical traditions, of those who have been "the friends of God."

The core conviction of this book is clear: that Christian spiritual formation, unlike other religious forms, is a personal reality grounded in the triune God of grace. It can be delegated only to disciples of Jesus who walk alongside other, perhaps less mature, followers of Christ. Books may help—otherwise this one would not have been written! But this book is to be discussed personally rather than merely read in isolation. For spiritual mentors matter most when the spiritual life is centered upon spiritual friendships. Read then this excellent book to become a wiser mentor of others, and read it to know what kind of person will help you most to become a more intimate friend of God.

The practicability of this book is simple yet deeply communicated. Living in the light of God's love, his divine personalness, requires us to grow in basic trust or *faith*—so central to the biblical message—as well as intimacy, the spirit of docility, responsiveness to divine grace, accountability and all else that we mean by biblical "righteousness." Then we shall enjoy what the Puritan divine Robert Bolton called "having a comfortable walk with God."

Reader, you are invited then in this book to enter into a deeper walk with God, as a sinner justified freely by his grace, to enjoy a fresh, living companionship in spiritual mentoring. If you bemoan the absence of a spiritual mentor in your life, then *be* one! This book will help you *be* what you long to *have*. It is to be more godly, more Christlike.

James M. Houston

Preface

This book emerged from conversations between the two authors as we shared our lives as spiritual mentors, Randy at North American Baptist Seminary, Sioux Falls, South Dakota, and Keith at Bethel College, St. Paul, Minnesota. We discovered a convergence of thinking and practice in our various responsibilities that drew us back to the writings of some of church history's great teachers and writers.

We have started the book with a descriptive outline of the book you hold in your hands. The Anderson/Reese Model of Spiritual Mentoring summarizes the teachings we have discovered through our own work and research and through the suggestive ideas of J. Robert Clinton, professor of leadership, School of World Mission, Fuller Theological Seminary, Pasadena, California.

The greatest value of this book, however, will be to return to this outline after you have spent time immersing yourself in the writing and histories of our guest list of classic spiritual writers. We hope this work provides a larger audience of readers an entree to some of their writings.

We are grateful to Dr. James Houston, former professor and chancellor of Regent College, Vancouver, British Columbia, for his kind encouragement and willingness to offer a profound foreword to this work.

Dr. Richard Sherry, an academic dean at Bethel College, carefully read and edited much of the grammar in several drafts of the work. Any other grammatical errors belong to the authors alone.

Randy's colleagues and students at North American Baptist Seminary helped shape the work by cheering encouragement, by reflecting critically over many cups of coffee and by allowing timely space for Randy to focus on the research and writing. Keith's mentors and students at Bethel College have touched his life as they have given grace and spoken truth to him.

The Anderson/Reese Model of Spiritual Mentoring

Definition of spiritual mentoring	*Spiritual mentoring is a triadic relationship between mentor, mentoree and the Holy Spirit, where the mentoree can discover, through the already present action of God, intimacy with God, ultimate identity as a child of God and a unique voice for kingdom responsibility. (See chapter two.)*
Distinctives of spiritual mentoring	■ *a means to enhance intimacy with God, ultimate identity and unique voice* ■ *a way to recognize the already present action of God in the mentoree's life* ■ *an effective model for personal development in character formation* ■ *an effective way to discern God's direction in decision-making* ■ *a historically proven diet for the journey of faith* ■ *an effective safeguard during boundary and transitional times in ministry*
Who is the mentor?	■ *one who creates a hospitable space of trust and intimacy* ■ *one who is able to discern the already present action of God in the mentoree* ■ *one who recognizes potential in people* ■ *one with an experience of spirituality who is affirmed by others for having a life worthy of emulation* ■ *one who seeks to live a life of authentic holiness, spiritual maturity, biblical knowledge and wisdom* ■ *one who is familiar with contemplative prayer, listening and other spiritual disciplines*
Who is the mentoree?	■ *one who desires spiritual growth and maturity* ■ *one who is vulnerable in sharing intimate issues of life* ■ *one who is responsive and respectful to the directives of the mentor* ■ *one who is teachable, submissive, faithful and obedient* ■ *one who desires to serve God with his or her life*

Movements in the Spiritual Mentoring Process

Attraction	*We define attraction as the initial establishment of the mentoring relationship. The tone is set by Augustine's challenge to the mentor, "Attract them by your way of life." Key components include claiming your own story as the mentor; initiation of the relationship primarily by the mentoree with a challenge for mentors to recognize potential mentorees; covenant making to establish motivation, frequency, location, format, accountability, confidentiality, evaluation and closure; potential relationships to avoid.*
Relationship	*We define relationship as the nurturing hospitable space of trust and intimacy. The life of the mentoree will more effectively be heard when a safe space is created by the mentor. Key components include: the respect of vulnerability and boundaries; seeing the mentoring relationship in the progressive stages of friendship of selection, probation, admission and harmony; recognizing the essential functions of holy listening, holy seeing and wholly listening.*
Responsiveness	*We define responsiveness as the sustaining of a responsive spirit of teachability. In order to grow, the mentoree must submit willingly to the guidance of the mentor. Various prayer movements, such as the "seven dwelling places" of Teresa of Ávila and the "dark night" of John of the Cross, are used to assist in fostering a spirit of responsiveness.*
Accountability	*We define accountability as growth through exercises of grace facilitated by the mentor. Ignatius sets the pace with spiritual exercises categorized as preparation of the heart, virtues of the heart, habits of the heart and rewards of the heart. Further suggestions include adaptable hospitality, intentionality and discipline, imagination, and discernment; Guyon's prayer through Scripture; the discipline of questions; and lectio divina.*
Empowerment	*We define empowerment as the discovery of one's unique voice for kingdom service that derives from intimacy with God and ultimate identity as a child of God. The mentoree discovers his or her unique voice in God's salvation story. The foundation is set in Scripture and validated through the classical perspectives.*

One

An Imitative Faith

He that followeth me walketh not in darkness, saith the Lord.
These are the words of Christ,
whereby we are admonished how we must imitate His life
and conversation if we would be truly enlightened
and delivered from all blindness of heart.[1]

THOMAS À KEMPIS

Christian faith is an imitative faith. It always has been. Beginning with Jesus' earliest words to the men and women who would become his apprentices of faith, Christianity has understood itself to be a faith taught by one to another. The life of Jesus Christ must be seen and held as the unique model worthy of imitation for Christians. "Jesus, then, is always the attractive source and challenging exemplar for Christian spirituality."[2]

"Follow me" may be the simplest description of Christian spirituality that exists anywhere, but the simplicity is deceptive. This simple command assumes a complex relationship through which one becomes educated for the reign of God.

That Jesus was a teacher in a world familiar with the relationship of rabbi and disciple is well documented. That Jesus was a "discipler" of others is also well understood. That Jesus intended a similar strategy for spiritual mentoring for the church is further enunciated in what is called "the Great Commission," in which it is clear that all disciples are intended to become teachers of faith to the nations:

Go therefore and make disciples of all nations . . . teaching them to obey everything that I have commanded you. (Mt 28:19-20)

Those who go are those who follow: this is the paradox of faith. Those who teach are those who have themselves been taught. The imitation of Christ, about which Thomas à Kempis wrote so eloquently in the fifteenth century, is a vision given to all disciples. We are forever students; we are forever taught. Each one who hears the words of Jesus, first to follow and then to go and teach others to obey, stands in a long line of disciples that originated with twelve followers hand-picked by Jesus, the rabbi-carpenter of Nazareth.

The kind of teaching Jesus provided them was very different from the classroom instruction of the academy today. It assumed a relationship and style that made different demands on both rabbi and disciple, teacher and learner, mentor and protégé. More like the work of the master craftsman tutoring the young apprentice, Jesus' style of instruction embodied a pedagogy that invested life in the learner through an incarnation of the message being taught. This teaching was not something that was conceptually defined for his disciples as much as it was lived, experienced, tasted and touched by the learners. Jesus not only spent time instructing, training and informing; he spent much time *forming a community.*

In the sweat of shared work as well as the dusty exertion of shared travel, they were always in the classroom. By the sea with wriggling, smelly and oily fish in their hands, in the fields with the crunch of fresh wheat snapped from stalks swaying in the hot Palestinian sun, even in the stimulation of the sensual barrage of the city with its crowds, bazaars, buildings, soldiers, markets—they were always in school, always becoming a community of learners whom he called disciples. "Follow me," he said to them. A world of meaning reverberates in the simple words of his call. Even the language of "call" is intensely related to Jesus' strategy of choosing, nurturing and developing an inner circle of disciples to whom he would give unique authority to teach the next generation of followers.

The great Christian apologist and missionary Paul of Tarsus clearly understood the imitative nature of this unique kind of education, for he said in 1 Thessalonians 1:6-7, "And *you became imitators* of us and of the Lord, for in spite of persecution you received the word with joy inspired by the Holy Spirit, so that *you became an example to all* the believers in Macedonia and in Achaia."

A further example of Paul's thinking is found in 2 Timothy 2:2, where we read the injunction "And what you have heard from me through many witnesses entrust to faithful people who will be able to teach others as well."

Later in the book of Acts, a man named Philip became the patron saint for us all as spiritual mentors as he came alongside a public official, a man who was bewildered reading the Scriptures. Philip's question is the simplest form known for the mentor: "Do you understand what you are reading?" The response of his Ethiopian friend is the cry for mentoring that resides in each one who wishes to go deeper into the Christian faith: "How can I, unless someone guides me?" (Acts 8:30-31). And a current translation of 1 John says, "This is the only way to be sure we're in God. Anyone who claims to be intimate with God ought to live the same kind of life Jesus lived" (1 Jn 2:5-6 The Message).

Spiritual formation, education of the heart, in other words, requires something more than traditional Western forms of instruction. It requires a mentorship of the heart, a relationship with a teacher of life who is able to convey what was learned from the teacher's own faithful mentor, a way of life that is formed, not merely instructions that are given. It requires a life shared by people who have learned that spiritual music is sung in its own way. To educate the heart requires learning that frees the imagination, prepares ears to listen, focuses eyes to look with attentiveness; it requires an open heart.

We contend that the rabbi-disciple relationship is not adequately understood as merely that of teacher-student or leader-follower but is more richly understood in the descriptive language of spiritual mentoring. Our common perspective as writers emerges from the vocation we share, that of teaching students in the academies of higher education, in college and seminary. Our working hours are occupied with the mission of educating people for the reign of God, which we recognize as incomplete without the intentional work of spiritual mentoring. As we challenge students to follow Jesus, we dare to say, "Imitate me as I seek to imitate Jesus; follow me as I seek to faithfully follow him." And we dare such temerity because others before us have dared such boldness in our own lives. Our lives have been profoundly influenced by those who are educators, though not always "teachers," mentors all, including parents, family, coworkers and spiritual friends.

Longing for More

There is a longing for spiritual navigation that broods in every Christian. We want to know the routes through the perilous courses of life. We want to know how we will reach our journey's end. We want a map or charts to guide us on the way. There is a yearning, however, that isn't satisfied by the normal fare of personal study, prayer and worship. It is a desire for more, a "more" that is impossible to define or explicate; it is a longing to know the richness of "the deeper life" or "mature faith" or "spiritual power." There are times we may simply try to increase our devotional disciplines to satisfy our longing by reading more and doing more but discover that the longing remains unsatisfied. At other times we turn to the latest technologies, books, tapes or conferences hoping to satisfy the longing for more, but to no avail. We come to the realization that we need help, that we are not meant to make this journey solo. We learn to listen to the voices of mentors, not as absolute experts with the final authoritative word but more as the shrewd and discerning expressions of those who have traveled this way before.

Keith first became aware of this when he was a college sophomore:

The prof knew something I didn't know and, though that didn't require a wealth of knowledge, I noticed it for the first time in my life and wanted to know something of the joyful harmony he found in the knowledge on which he feasted with such gusto. His love for the study of American history, which was eventually to become my own interest, left an echo ringing in my soul. It was the first time in my life that I sensed that the music of the mind could sound so beautiful. He would become one of those few people in my life whose impact can never be measured or described to anyone else. It has to be heard with the ears of one's individual experience. As it happened, he became a spiritual mentor as well, a voice of spiritual encouragement, one who validated my nascent attempts in the frightening (to me) world of pastoral ministry. I hardly noticed that he was doing it, but now I can see it like a billboard with eight-foot letters naming the obvious: "This man invested himself in you; he gave some part of his life and time to the nurture of your spirit; he freed your mind to long for more."

A seminary professor was more direct—he let me know that there was some work to be done to prepare me for a life in the ministry and that he would be one of those who would help me create some foundational strength in my emerging leadership. And so we met nearly weekly for three years in time. His oft-repeated greeting to me was

"You need to come and see me!" Though the conversations are different now, we still meet frequently. He taught me to listen to truth echoing within my own life as I listened even more attentively to the culture and truth of the Bible.

Randy's early encounter with a wise spiritual mentor came while he was in the beginning stages of discerning his own call for vocational ministry:

Leaving behind the tool pouch from my journeyman electrician days in northern Canada to travel across North America with seventeen others in a church-related ministry team seemed like a daring adventure to discern if I was indeed "called" to the ministry. Although I was satisfied with serving God as an electrician, there was an undeniable longing for something more in my faith journey. In the context of serving others I began to see glimmers of hope that perhaps I too could "leave my nets" and follow Christ in full-time service. However, the hope became short-lived as echoes from my past seemed to confirm my colorful weaknesses, as well as the obvious fact that I didn't have the proper skills and talents for such a task. Better stay with the nets—in my case, my electrician's tool pouch.

I especially admired John for his ability to make space for those he was given charge of leading. John was not one to dish out grand measures of advice, but he had an uncanny ability to help you listen to your own life. In that hospitable and safe space John created for me, I began to listen to my life like I had never done before. In a priestly fashion he listened to story after story from my life, stories I knew were validating weaknesses that would keep me from being successful in the ministry. To my surprise, John didn't agree with my self-perception. He also did not prescribe a penance of more prayer, more biblical study or more service. Rather, he simply led me to recognize God's amazing threads of grace at work in my life that formed a tapestry like none other. John helped me recognize I had a story to share—my story—and a song to sing—my song. Those perceived weaknesses would soon become strengths through which I would discover the unique voice God had given to me to use for God's kingdom purposes.

In the course of our own faith journeys these people helped us listen to things we couldn't hear on our own. Our search for more required their help to move us further along than we could on our own. Their voices helped us discover the empowering truth that God was already at work in our lives inviting us to a greater intimacy as beloved children and empowering us to discover our own unique voices. It was the beginning of something that we might call community or *koinonia* through spiritual direction. It was the realization that began to pulse within us until we saw that crucial seasons of growth depend somehow on those with whom we choose to spend our time. We needed time with those who knew what we only wished we could know; their fluency (as it sounded to us) made us painfully aware of our illiteracy and of our longing to know the taste of those words in our own mouths.

Learning the Language of Faith

Just as we learn a new language best by immersion in the culture in which it is spoken, so, we believe, are people formed spiritually by an immersion in the culture in which faith is lived in heart and experience. We hang out at the dock where the old sailors are. We watch them on their ships and learn the nautical language which they use as easily as their mother tongue. We listen to their stories and learn the lore that is part of the legacy of the sea. Nothing compares to listening to them describe that with which they are exuberantly, passionately in love.

You can learn to speak a foreign language by sitting alone in a room, reciting grammar and memorizing vocabulary cards, but you will never know the rich taste of the language on your tongue until you hear it spoken by others who love the language and speak it with a fluency rich in the experience of their own lives. The way to nurture our lives of faith most deeply is by spending time with experienced and wise mentors who can help us discover the way, to read stories of the great men and women of faith who preceded us in the body of Christ.

For Reflection

Take a moment at this time and look at your own life and ask:

☐ Who has created a safe space in which to tell my own story?

☐ Who has already been a mentor for me? Was it a pastor, teacher, authority figure or parent, friend or peer?

☐ Whose "song of faith" has rung most powerfully in my life?
☐ Whose life do I desire to imitate or emulate?

Unlikely Mentors of the Soul

It is significant that the word *person* (*persona* in Latin) comes from the Greek word *prosopon*, which can be translated "face to face." In other words, each human is a person as he or she stands face to face, turned toward another person, engaged in dialogue, involved in relationship. In contrast, the word *individual*, developed centuries after the word *person*, comes from the Latin word *individuus*, "not divisible." These derivations offer us important clues to understand how we grow. We are persons, face to face, in community, not separated individuals; we are a people in community who need others to bring us to spiritual maturity. We discover our identity in the context of community. We learn best *together*, with the help of other people.

Think yet again about the wise voices of your own life, those persons whom you encountered face to face. Did they include the unlikely voices of those who were the least educated and seemed least qualified for teaching you the depths of life? Not all of the teachers or mentors of our lives are those who would recognize themselves as educators of spiritual formation.

Every day Keith would meet the man at the dumpster on the loading dock in the building where Keith worked as a young college student:

> His name was Chuck, and we were as different in background as two men could be. I was a young man on my way through "higher education," an inflated term if the goal is to develop persons; he was near retirement and had an eighth-grade education. I was of the privileged middle class; he was not. I am white. He is African-American. I grew up in the northern city and suburbs of Chicago, he in the rural south. He was the custodian whose job all day was to empty the baskets of "important" people and to throw out the trash for these busy and influential people, decision-makers whose choices would make or break the fortunes of the company. But Chuck was a man who had something I came to cherish—commonsense wisdom that grew out of his faith and his life experience. He was a sage, a seer, a wise man who could see more deeply into life than most I have ever known since that time. In time we opened to one another, and he taught me much as we met on

the dock for my "lessons" in wisdom. He didn't set out to teach me, much less to mentor me, but he did both because, in his soul, he was a teacher and a mentor whose wisdom was given voice in a southern accent spoken in a northern city. His words didn't add much information to my own ongoing education in theology, but they continue to shape me as a person to this day.

So are you shaped by your own face-to-face experiences with the many unlikely voices whose faith has mentored your own, whose wisdom has been shared, whose discernment you have heeded, and most of all, whose words have helped you listen well to your life. In this book we will invite you to understand spiritual mentoring as a ministry given to each of us as we live in our families, in our friendships, in our churches, on our jobs and in all places we find ourselves. Spiritual mentoring is far too important to be left in the hands of a few with special credentials and certification; the nurture of the spirit belongs to the baptized, to the church writ large, to the priesthood of all the believers.

The Great Cloud of Witnesses

Did Jesus' form of teaching, discipling or mentoring meet only a short-term need for a specific time and place in church history? We say no. We believe that spiritual mentoring was given for the church throughout history. The forms may vary and the styles may change, but each one of the faithful yearns for a mentor who will come alongside as a companion on the journey.

There are voices of the past that need to be heard today. These voices evoke rather than explain, educe rather than instruct. They offer an *invitation* and an *initiation*. We are *invited* to participate with them in a conversation with a history that is shared by all who follow Jesus. In fact, discipleship is always practiced by those who come after Jesus through a long line of others who followed him before we did. Thus we are *initiated* into this family of witnesses, those who traveled this way before us and, in some mystical sense, observe us, even now. These are "the great cloud of witnesses" described in the book of Hebrews. Elizabeth A. Dreyer calls theirs "the living faith of the dead."[3]

Tilden Edwards's descriptive word choices highlights the weighty need for giving attention to the voices of our common, historical past. "Christian tradition is the *lived* and *tested* experience and *reflection* of a diverse body of people over time united by a *commitment* to approach the purpose and way of life through the lineage of Jesus Christ" (emphasis added).[4] These four words are descriptive of the process: *lived, tested, reflected* and *committed.*

There is great danger for us in the historical amnesia that prevails in the church today. If things are contemporary, computer-driven or "seeker-effective," then we are apt to read them and get excited. Maybe that's the problem—we get excited by fads and trends and forget our identity as the body of Christ. The classical voices of our past call us back to that foundational identity.

Even the word *classical* carries different meanings. For some it refers to the music of an earlier "classical" era when symphonic music was the standard. For some it refers to the "golden" era of rock 'n' roll some ten or twenty or thirty years ago. We have, however, a rich gold mine of classical Christian literature that has been *lived,* has been *tested,* is *reflective* of a diverse body of people over time and is *committed* to the way of life of Jesus. It is rightly deserving of the designation "classical" thought.

To follow Jesus means that we follow these companions of the past, for no one comes to faith alone; we come to faith as we follow those who followed at an earlier time. Hebrews 12 speaks of these particular companions of the past as "so great a cloud of witnesses," evoking the image of an Olympic arena in which weary athletes are cheered on by former Olympians whose own races preceded them. Those who are in the race now are applauded, cheered and encouraged by the audience of witnesses whose own earlier races inspire the runners today. The names cited in Hebrews form a roster of women and men who followed Jesus and whose lives mentored the succeeding generations of faith. But look at these athletes of faith. They were imperfect, failed and fallen as well as bold, courageous, faithful and strong. We dare not look for perfect examples of faith or wait in the illusion that we will arrive soon at our own perfection. Instead we will find our souls freed for growth when we learn to listen to the very human, imperfect voices of the great cloud of saints.

Companions of the Past

Unless we listen to the voices of our companions of the past, the timbre of our own voices will never be as rich, the depth as profound, the echoes as sonorous. In fact, until we hear the voices of the past, it is unlikely we will truly hear "the Word," for as Paul articulates with precision and economy, the past provides a sacramental power for the present: "For I received *[paralam-bano]* from the Lord what I also handed on to you, that the Lord Jesus on the night when he was betrayed took a loaf of bread, and when he had given thanks, he broke it and said, 'This is my body that is for you. Do this in remembrance of me' " (1 Cor 11:23-24).

Paul insists the church in Corinth must understand the great "*paralambano* principle": "I *received* from the Lord what I also *handed on* to you." *Paralambano* is a technical word for the transmission of tradition from one person to another, from the past to the future, from those who first lived the inaugurating experience to those who will continue to experience it in the remembering of it. In the *paralambano* moments of our lives we hear echoes of those companions of the past that somehow create moments of sacrament in our lives. In the receiving and passing on of the traditions of the faith, grace is poured into a common present moment.

Gerard Manley Hopkins described holiness as the "dearest freshness deep down things."[5] The bread becomes a living experience with Christ in the spiritual mystery of the communion, so the tradition of the past becomes a living grace for the church today. The cup becomes a living experience of the resurrected Christ, mentoring becomes a carrier in the present moment. We receive from the Lord what we have learned and then pass on the powerfully present word of the Lord to others.

The past is re-membered in the lives of the next generation of the faithful who will do the same for the generation that follows them. It is the biblical means of conserving a living historic faith. Walter Brueggemann says, "Every community that wants to last beyond a single generation must concern itself with education."[6] But it is education of a very particular kind that will keep alive a community and create a body of faith in the next generation; it is education of the soul, spiritual mentoring for spiritual formation.

Spiritual direction is a centuries-old means of spiritual formation. Early in the life of the church, the work of spiritual direction was taken seriously and carefully developed. Before there were programs for Sunday school, Christian education, catechism classes or Bible study, there was a practice of mentoring in which the great cloud of witnesses handed on to the next generation the truth and power of the life of faith. Sometimes this took a particular form called spiritual direction. Even a cursory glance at comments from early Christians will reveal their commitment and practice of "handing on" what they "received from the Lord": Gregory Nazianzen (330-387) tells us "direction is the greatest of all sciences." Augustine (354-430) believed "no one can walk without a guide."[7]

Spiritual direction is generally associated with the monastic movement, believed to have been founded by Anthony, who died in A.D. 356. In the fourth and fifth centuries the desert mystics understood the spiritual director as a father who helped to shape the inner lives of his sons through prayer, concern and pastoral care. Later in Western Christianity Gregory said, "The art of ruling souls is the art of arts."[8] In the fourteenth century Catherine of Siena became spiritual director to a circle of friends, her *bella brigada*, to whom she wrote numerous letters of guidance. Spiritual direction involved men and women, clergy and laity, educated and illiterate, young and old.

Jean Grou, a Jesuit writing in 1731-1803, offered a manual for interior souls in which he said, "To direct a soul is to lead it in the ways of God, it is to teach the soul to listen for the Divine inspiration, and to respond to it."[9]

The practice of spiritual guidance has always been part of Protestant spiritual practices, although the language of spiritual direction has not always been a major part of Protestant vocabulary. Zwingli advised that Christians should confess to God alone, but if it seemed necessary, the Christian should consult a wise counselor. John Calvin was referred to as a "director of souls," and Richard Baxter, writing to other Puritans in 1656, listed four groups of people who needed special attention: the immature, those with a particular corruption, declining Christians and the strong. The last group, he declared, need the greatest care.

Over the centuries then, the practice of spiritual direction has always existed in the life of Christian communities. Not always central to its spirituality but always essential to the spiritual formation of some, spiritual direction has a long and noble history of practice in the development of spirituality in the lives of people. While we can define spirituality in dozens of complex and intricate ways, we wish to begin by calling the church to listen to its own heartbeat. What is this spirituality that spiritual mentors will seek to develop in the lives of the learner and mentoree?

Learning to Attend to the Presence of God in Everything

When we pay attention to the stop sign at the corner, we take it seriously and change our behavior because it is there. We see it, we notice it, and then we adapt our lifestyle accordingly. Spirituality is practical: everything can be seen as a container of the holy. In fact, the everyday containers of time and place become holy as God's presence fills them. Spirituality is, therefore, inherently and intensely sacramental. We understand that God's presence is not confined to that which is sacred; rather God's grace is mediated through the ordinary. It is experiential rather than abstract. As an old Russian proverb says, "Every day can be a messenger of God."

All men and women of faith long for their lives to be immersed in the holy. The dull ache of routine causes us to become inured to the wonders about us. Gerald Manley Hopkins wrote that "the world is charged with the grandeur of God."[10] The experience of God, in other words, is present in the world around us. Our world is saturated with grace-giving, wonder-evoking moments. Jesus said early in his ministry "the kingdom of heaven has come near" (Mt 4:17). He declared that it is near, present, historical, though incomplete and awaiting fulfillment. The Irish poet Yeats saw truth as something similarly gritty and physical: "God guard me from those thoughts men think / In the mind alone; / He that sings a lasting song / Thinks in a marrow-bone."[11]

Barbara Brown Taylor tells her story of eyes opening to God's light after hearing a sermon as a young child. Her words relate the practical implications of understanding spirituality:

> My friend's words changed everything for me. I could no longer see myself or the least detail in my life in the same way again. When the service was over that day, I walked out of it into a God-enchanted world, where I could not wait to find further clues to heaven on earth. Every leaf, every ant, every shiny rock called out to me—begging to be watched, to be listened to, to be handled and examined. I became a detective of divinity, collecting evidence of God's genius and admiring the tracks left for me to follow."[12]

Spiritual mentoring includes a process of listening to the life of another and then teaching people to open their eyes and see what is there—every-where—teaching them to become detectives for the presence of divinity.

For Whom Is This Book Written?
☐ It is written for those who desire to find a spiritual mentor and want help.
☐ It is written for those who have been invited to become a spiritual mentor

for another and want help.

☐ It is written for those who hunger for something more in their journeys of faith.

We write to mentor and mentoree alike asking a singular and monumental question: How does one become spiritually formed through mentoring? We call this book *Spiritual Mentoring: A Guide for Seeking and Giving Direction* because we have discovered that a relationship with a spiritual mentor is one of the best ways to progress in the lifelong work of spiritual formation. We have become convinced that the answer to the question asked above can be discovered in a creative attention to those mentors who have journeyed ahead of us. We invite you to be a part of creative conversations with some of the best voices in this arena of spiritual mentoring. You might imagine yourself sitting down with a cup of coffee in hand as you converse with these biblical, historical and contemporary sources in a creative dialogue about faith.

Daniel 12:3 offers a gentle hint of how highly the role of the mentor is valued. The work of the wise voice that instructs others in justice is likened to the very stars of heaven: "Those who are wise shall shine like the brightness of the sky, and those who lead many to righteousness, like the stars forever and ever."

Our foundational purpose in this book is to propose a historically informed vision for the contemporary work of spiritual mentoring. Our core conviction is that spiritual formation is nurtured most profoundly when disciples are "apprenticed" to a spiritual mentor who will partner with God's Holy Spirit toward spiritual development.

We have written first to mentors and then to mentorees letters that we hope will inspire and challenge both. Intended as words of encouragement with realism for both, these letters will summarize some of the material that follows in the book.

Letter to a Would-Be Mentor from the Authors

You have been asked to become a mentor to another. There are few honors in life more precious than to walk alongside a brother or sister on a journey of spiritual formation. If you feel overwhelmed and doubt your worthiness for the task, this is a good sign that you are ready and may be qualified, for the ministry of a mentor begins with humility. You may feel something akin to great unworthiness and are likely to exclaim, "Who am I that anyone should emulate me? I know my own flaws and failures, my contradictions, far too well, and the passions within that rise up in unholiness, as well as moments of holiness. And yet I feel the joyfulness of opportunity—maybe I could help this friend listen to life. I know that I can ask some pertinent questions and can help this friend think through these questions."

Probe your motivation: Why would you agree to fill this role in someone's life? If there is a desire to have power over another, perhaps it is time to think again. Mentoring is not about you; it is about the other. If there is a desire to instruct and tutor another in the ways that you have found useful, perhaps it is time to think again. Mentoring is not about telling. It is about listening—to the Holy Spirit and to the life of the other. If there is a desire for status or position in the eyes of others, you will surely fail, for mentoring is a servant's role. It is true that there are times of instructing, guiding and sharing of wisdom, but mentoring is primarily about discernment and learning to recognize where God is already present and active in the heart of the other.

Spiritual mentoring is uniquely relational for it invites many others into the circle of conversation—voices of the past in Scripture and church tradition, voices of the present in teachers and wise guides, voices of the heart in the Holy Spirit and in the heart of your mentoree. If your need is to create a duplicate of yourself, remember that the God who makes each snowflake unique has likewise made each person unique. Your experience belongs to the particularities of your own history; do not impose it on another, but let God form the other as distinctly as God formed you.

Are you able to create a safe space for hospitality where the mentoree can allow the masks of life to be shed in order to discover the freedom of authentic conversation? Are you able to practice the spiritual discipline of confidentiality that you might protect your friend's dignity and pain? You may hold in your hands words of failure, struggle, disbelief, doubt, discouragement, despair, brokenness, inadequacy, negligence and delinquency. You may have information that can hurt or help your friend but cannot be shared unless they give you permission. Are you as trustworthy as you desire in the trust you would give your own spiritual mentor?

If you require precision, order, sequential progression and careful forward motion, then you will be sorely disappointed, for spiritual mentoring is messy because life is messy, disorderly and random. The great master of ceremonies may be at work behind the scenes, as C. S. Lewis envisioned in *The Four*

Loves, but often the drama on center stage is chaotic, unrehearsed and confused. The turbulence of normal life can upset and dismay, but it is in such messiness that order will surprise and design will chase away randomness.

A commitment of time is necessary for spiritual mentoring. Time to listen to life together for the rhythm of God's movement and time to listen to life alone, when each of you will meet in the space of reflective thought. Are you able to give time to your friend? There are days when spiritual mentoring seems a quiet, wasteful way to spend an hour or two. The conversation is often about little things rather than grand things. The pace is often pensive and slow. The process is sometimes stuttering, for there are large silent spaces in the conversation of reflection, but in such hours, souls are freed to sing.

You have been invited to participate in a walk through the calendar of daily life where God is not always immediately visible to the human eye, which is why you are needed, to help your friend pay attention. And what will he or she see? There will be three primary themes or empowerments you will watch for in order to develop the ever-unfolding story of your friend's life: intimacy with God, ultimate identity as a beloved child of God and a unique voice for kingdom responsibility. Everything we do is lived under the canopy of these three defining questions that have been the baseline questions asked throughout all of biblical history; they are the trail markers for your work as a spiritual mentor. A simple way to remember these three is through the use of three paradigmatic questions:

☐ Who is God?

☐ Who am I?

☐ What am I to do with my life?

Letter from the Authors to One Seeking a Mentor

You are about to embark on a journey of great possibilities for your growth. You have carefully considered your desire to find a spiritual mentor as a guide and spiritual companion. You find yourself asking questions that reflect a longing for more in your journey of faith. You might be helped to know that there are not universal "steps" to follow because this is a process of wise discernment, not of following a recipe. You will want to begin with prayer, seeking God's help for a mentor who will stand alongside you as spiritual friend. Wait for God to direct you to a name, a church, a friend or a group. Perhaps a pastor, your church or other friends can help introduce you to people who are willing and prepared for the work of spiritual mentoring. When you have gained some confidence that you have discerned God's direction for you, take the step and act on your discernment.

But you also need to know this is a time of great spiritual danger, and the caution flags must be observed as urgently as the crew of a ship on the water watch for signs of rocks below the surface. You have been directed to another whom you identify as a person you can trust, a person of integrity and wisdom, a person in whom you believe. The temptation is to see this person as one with answers to give, rather than presence to share, solutions to provide or questions to ponder. Your mentor is human and imperfect. If you believe otherwise, you will endow your friend with a spiritual authority no human being should be given.

This is a time in which you will assess *your* readiness to share your journey and its many stories with another who has the potential to shame you, hurt you or otherwise embarrass you. There is risk in spiritual mentoring, so be cautious in the selection process. Don't be in a hurry to find a mentor; instead, wait on God's Spirit to help direct you to one whom God has chosen for you. And then bring all the readiness, openness, willingness, curiosity and responsiveness you can, for these will be your greatest contribution to the process of your own spiritual formation.

You will need to be ready for tedium. Growth usually happens not with great speed but with great depth, not with hurried steps but with a deliberate gait, not in the style of Fast Cash machines or Instant Breakfast but in the style of creation that knows patient time. If you're looking for immediate results, quick changes and a speedy make-over, then you'll have to go to the mall, where such things are sold to those gullible enough to buy them. Spirituality is not quick and easy because spirituality is about participating in the learning process of life itself, richly cultivated and nourished. The impulsiveness of our culture creates the drifting that characterizes so many instead of the settledness that comes from a solid anchor of the soul. The business of soul making requires an intentional pause along the way to look and to listen, to wonder and ponder, to contemplate and reflect.

Last of all, we want to remind you that the work ahead of you will require of you the development of an open heart. When Solomon was given his one wish from the Lord, he asked for a *lave shemiah*, which is usually translated from the Hebrew language as "wisdom" but means, as well, an "open heart." To be an effective mentor one must learn to listen. To be effectively mentored, one must develop equally well an openness of heart and a sincere desire to be "transformed by the renewing of your mind" (Rom 12:2), "to hunger and thirst after righteousness" (Mt 6:33), to listen to the voice of God, over and over, day by day, again and again, until you will hear it with the freshness of new ears and see it with the eyes of a newborn child.

There will be three primary themes or empowerments to be developed in the ever-unfolding story of your life: intimacy with God, ultimate identity as the beloved of God and a unique voice for kingdom responsibility. Everything we do in the work of spiritual formation is lived under the canopy of these three defining questions. A simple way to remember these three is through the use of three questions:

☐ Who is God?

☐ Who am I?

☐ What am I to do with my life?

The Guest List

In order to better listen to your own life, we will tell the stories and illuminate the lives of seven men and women who have much to teach us. They will become our conversation partners and mentors through the pages ahead.

Augustine was a fourth-century African monastic theologian whose vulnerable authenticity provided hope to others seeking reflections of grace for their own journey.

Aelred of Rievaulx was a twelfth-century exemplar of spiritual friendship whose articulation of the mentoring relationship went well beyond the scope of those before and after him.

Julian of Norwich was a fourteenth-century Englishwoman whose ministry of mentoring created intense intimacy with God, flowing out of who she was, not out of the dictates of a special role or office.

Ignatius of Loyola was a sixteenth-century convert whose apostolic influence was expressed in spiritual mentoring, through which growth, maturity and discernment for service to God were discovered.

Teresa of Ávila, a sixteenth-century Spanish woman, was sought out as a spiritual mentor by many who desired a deeper sense of God's reality in their lives.

John of the Cross was a sixteenth-century intellectual whose mentoring guided many through the dark night of the soul toward greater union and intimacy with God.

Jeanne Guyon, a seventeenth-century French widow, was sought out for her spiritual mentoring that resulted in an authentic spiritual freedom among those who were shackled by their religious trappings.

At first glance, these mentors of the faith may seem outdated and certainly not *en vogue* with the faith questions of the contemporary Christian. Do not be fooled, for they cherished their own spiritual formation processes, and the stories of their journeys raise some of the premier questions for the Christian community today: How do I take the next step in my journey of faith? Who will help me get there? We encourage you not to be in a hurry to discover a formula or program; instead we suggest that you listen to and through the experience of this great cloud of witnesses from the history of the Christian church. Their words will deeply impress the practice of mentoring upon your mind and heart.

Further Reflection for the Mentor

1. What motivates you to participate in the ministry of spiritual mentoring? From what does the desire to mentor another derive?

2. Can you remember significant moments of growth in your own life that were prompted by a relationship with one whom you consider a mentor?

3. As you read the letter to a mentor, what responses emerge for you? What does it evoke in your own soul? Do you feel ready to be a mentor to another?

4. What are the areas of spiritual growth prompted for you in this chapter?

5. How have you been affirmed toward a ministry of spiritual mentoring?

Further Reflection for the Mentoree

1. What motivates you at this time in your life to seek out another to be a mentor for you?

2. Have you had significant moments of growth in your life previously that were prompted by a mentor?

3. As you read the letter to one seeking a mentor, what responses emerge for you?

4. What do you imagine might happen in your life if you begin a spiritual mentoring relationship?

5. What are the areas of spiritual growth prompted for you in this chapter?

Two

Reading Between the Lines
What Is Spiritual Mentoring?

The whole purpose of spiritual direction is to penetrate beneath the surface
of a man's life, to get behind the facade of conventional gestures
and attitudes which he presents to the world,
and to bring out his inner spiritual freedom, his inmost truth,
which is what we call the likeness of Christ in his soul.[1]

THOMAS MERTON

Jeanne Guyon was born in 1648 France. A brief fifteen years later she was married to an invalid twenty-three years her senior, and at an early age she became a wealthy widow. At that point she began exploring the life of prayer and spiritual intimacy through spiritual guidance. Her search eventually led her to write with simple elegance of intimacy with God. This intimacy called for a dying to self and being consumed with the passionate love of God, which gave a new awareness of true identity as a believer.[2] These same writings led to her eventual arrest under the reign of Louis XIV, where she was "denounced as a heretic and imprisoned, eventually in the infamous Bastille."[3] What motivated her heart was a desire to know God intimately and to teach others how to grow into that same kind of intimate relationship. Through her writings she started a ministry of spiritual mentoring in the seventeenth century that has continued throughout the history of the church. The writings of Madame Guyon have been widely read for three hundred years. Her understanding of spiritual guidance is a powerful place to begin our study of the nature of spiritual mentoring.

Her historically influential writing *Experiencing the Depths of Jesus Christ* focused on the connection between mentoring and intimacy with God. Guyon taught that a mentor was to be concerned with issues of the heart with a primary focus on the emotional dimension of the mentoree's development. She emphasized the essential need for sincerity, authenticity and the establishment of trust, all of which are fundamentals for the stage of attraction. She also recognized that growing toward intimacy with God created a sense of acceptance, safety and courage. The mentoree was able to define himself or herself as a beloved child of God. She believed that personal renewal in intimacy with God was the basis for renewal in the church, as well as renewal in motivation to live out the truths of the gospel for those yet to be converted. Perhaps no other book has been as widely read as a call to intimacy with God. Written primarily for uneducated peasants, her words compelled people to move into a living experience of Jesus Christ.

In this chapter we want to introduce you to the concept of the nature of spiritual mentoring in that kind of living experience with Christ and show how it is different from spiritual direction. We will offer a foundational description of the distinctive characteristics of spiritual mentoring and suggest some of the essential skills and attributes needed to be an effective mentor. Although we will outline these as lists, spiritual mentoring does not proceed according to a schema or series of steps; instead it is a sensitive movement of paying attention to God, to self and to the life of the mentoree by both mentor and mentoree. It is a dynamic and wise relationship that discerns next steps to take in the journey of faith.

For Reflection

As you begin this chapter, take a moment to ponder your own emerging definition of spiritual mentoring.

☐ What are the necessary movements in spiritual mentoring?

☐ How does one proceed as a mentor?

☐ What are the requisite skills and qualities of one who would become a mentor?

Renewal Through Spiritual Mentoring

At the present time spiritual mentoring is emerging as one of the brightest hopes for the spiritual vitality of the church. People are hungry for the relationships that mentoring provides, so they seek out wise persons who can become those mentors for them. The movement toward mentoring in business, education and health care adds yet another catalyst for the current renewal of attention to *spiritual* mentoring. In many corners of the Christian world, there is a climate of interest in the role that spiritual mentoring might play in the development of spirituality. There has even been renewed interest in the work done by the ancient guilds where a young apprentice was nurtured and trained by a more experienced artisan. Theological institutions are assessing their effectiveness in the formation of Christian leaders, only to realize their neglect of the type of mentoring that attends to the spiritual formation of the emerging leader. Doctrinal astuteness, proper exegetical practice and the implementation of the latest growth strategy can no longer be considered the complete list of ingredients for the making of a "successful" minister who will lead the church.

The term *mentor* actually comes from the world of Greek mythology. Ulysses placed his son Telemachus under the tutelage and care of a wise sage named Mentor. Ulysses was away fighting in the Trojan War, so Mentor was responsible for teaching young Telemachus "not only in book learning but also in the wiles of the world."[4] Mentor's task was to provide an education of soul and spirit as well as mind, an education in wisdom and not merely in information.

Historically, spiritual direction tended to share several of the following five characteristics in classical Christianity:

a. structured/formal
b. hierarchical and one-directional (top-down)
c. authoritarian (tended to be "directive")
d. "official" and clerical
e. individualistic and private

By contrast, the interest today includes curiosity about new forms of spiritual guidance and methods of spiritual instruction, which tend to share several of the contrasting five characteristics:

a. informal
b. mutual
c. suggestive and evocative rather than directive
d. unofficial, more lay than clergy, many people involved in "unsanctioned" work
e. small group settings, as well as individualized

Several different names have been used across the centuries for the concept of the mentoring relationship that gives attention to the development of one's spirituality. What we are calling spiritual mentoring has also been referred to as spiritual counsel, spiritual direction, soul-friendship, discipling and simply spiritual guidance. We have chosen the term *spiritual mentoring* for any of these forms of guided spiritual formation that are practiced today. These relationships may be formal or informal, structured or unstructured, hierarchical or mutual, but they all have one primary function: they are processes of spiritual formation by which one person becomes a spiritual guide for one or several others. These may include the accidental and *ad hoc* moments of spiritual formation as well as the planned and intentional appointments for spiritual formation. It is our conviction that the quiet work of spiritual mentoring in its myriad forms offers a renewed pathway to the development of exceptional Christian leaders and the spiritual formation of true imitators of Jesus' way to spiritual wholeness.

The technical term for a spiritual seeker working in an intentional relationship with a spiritual mentor is mente, directee, or protégé. Each of these has a formal, stiff or technical affect for many. We have chosen to use the term *mentoree* except in our descriptions of the historical and classical writings, where we will use the terms chosen by the classical writers themselves.

The work of J. Robert Clinton helpfully suggests that mentoring can be understood in a variety of *relational* roles and types, as shown in table 1.[5] (See appendix 1 for additional characteristics of Clinton's nine types of mentoring relationships.)

This list is suggestive of the many kinds of relationships mentors might have with people. Mentoring does not come in a one-size-fits-all package. Mentors and mentoring are as unique as the individual relationship. Spiritual mentoring is the work of the entire body of Christ. Spiritual mentoring, then, obviously welcomes a style that is unique to each relationship we are privileged to help grow in faith. From whom and how that spiritual nurture comes is less important than that it comes.

In our research and writing, we asked several foundational questions about the role spiritual mentoring can play in spiritual formation:

☐ What can we learn from both the ancients and contemporary writers?

☐ What can we comprehend from the past centuries that can be applied to the more informal style of mentoring emerging today?

☐ What can we discern biblically?

☐ What can we discover historically?

Our conclusion is overwhelming: One of the processes that strongly assists in spiritual formation is the informal model of spiritual mentoring. Mentoring is one of the most influential ways to help us grow into intimacy with

Type of mentoring relationship	Function of the mentoring relationship
Discipler	seeks empowerment for the basic discipleship functions in following Christ
Spiritual Guide	provides accountability for spirituality and the practice of spiritual disciplines for spiritual growth and maturity
Coach	enhances skill development for ministry, as well as the motivation to use the developed skills
Counselor	gives timely advice and perspective to a protégé for viewing life and ministry
Teacher	imparts knowledge and motivation for its implementation in the life of the mentoree
Sponsor	offers career guidance and protection as an emerging leader advances in a ministry setting
Contemporary Model	provides a personal model for life and ministry that commands emulation
Historical Model	a (passive) way of learning principles and values for life and ministry from former leaders
Divine Contact	offers timely guidance or discernment perceived as divine intervention

Table 1. A variety of types and functions in mentoring relationships

God, accept our identity as the beloved of God and discover our unique voices for kingdom responsibility. It is now time to define the process we have called spiritual mentoring. We have identified seven essential elements of the ministry of spiritual mentoring.

1. The Incarnate Word: Spiritual Mentoring Is Relational
Definitions of spiritual direction abound in the literature of classical historic Christian writers. Some are narrow and specific; some are broad and generic. All agree on one starting premise: Spiritual mentoring is a relationship. Whether that relationship is formal and structured, informal and casual, consistent or sporadic, the heart of spiritual mentoring is relational.

The life of Jesus Christ and its call, "follow me," must certainly be experienced as a call to teach *what* he taught and to teach *as* he taught. Spiritual mentoring will seek to follow Jesus in content and style, in message and method, and in substance and form. The theological term for Jesus' ministry is *incarnational,* a word that means "enfleshed" or "embodied." In simple terms Jesus' life *became* his message. He revealed in his life what he said in his words. The incarnationally relational style that Jesus chose becomes the form we describe as spiritual mentoring. His inner life of passionate intimacy with his Father becomes the great paradigm for all who would follow him in the development of disciples for the kingdom. Jesus' methodology presents a challenge to the present-day culture of productivity, which demands a speedy programmatic approach for the process of making disciples.

Jesus' method is taught most directly in the biblical text of the Gospel of John. Its probable author, John the apostle, is often described as "the one whom Jesus loved" (Jn 13:23). The words penned by the apostle are crafted to present a coupled message of intimacy and incarnation. In the first chapter are recorded the words that can be held as a simple, yet profound missiological method—a method motivated by the love of Christ.

> The true light, which enlightens everyone, was coming into the world. He was in the world, and the world came into being through him; yet the world did not know him. He came to what was his own, and his own people did not accept him. But to all who received him, who believed in his name, he gave power to become children of God, who were born, not of blood or of the will of the flesh or of the will of man, but of God. And the Word became flesh and lived among us, and we have seen his glory, the glory as of a father's only son, full of grace and truth. (Jn 1:9-14)

The longed-for Messiah came incarnationally to live among us (literally, to "pitch his tent") for a while. The resounding message is one of redemption through the incarnated Christ. Now all nations will have opportunity to experience the intimate love of God, which provides privileged status as empowered, loved children of God. Being incarnational means "pitching one's tent" among those who need to hear and experience the intimate love of God. It is the foundational example of relationality in spiritual mentoring. It is a relationality that begins with one's own relationship with God and then moves toward relationship with others.

2. Grounded in the Ordinary: Spiritual Mentoring Is Autobiographical

A second foundational understanding is that spiritual mentoring is autobiographical. The mentoring relationship gives us the opportunity to explore boldly the life of another. In fact, the success or effectiveness of spiritual mentoring may be directly related to the ability of mentor and mentoree to move beneath the surface into the depths of treasures within the mentoree. Anything that we bring to the surface has the potential to turn out to be silver or gold hidden in the rough, angular and random shapes of the earthly rock containers that carry these unique treasures. The patient, sometimes tedious work of mining for the rich treasures within the seemingly worthless rocks is the work of spiritual mentoring. These rocks are the stories of our daily lives.

Those whose writings on spirituality or spiritual direction have influenced the church over the centuries have often understood the sacredness of ordinary time, ordinary life, ordinary events. Within the mundane life, precious metal can be mined and refined. Perhaps no one has described this methodology more succinctly than Eugene Peterson, who said, "Pastoral work . . . is that aspect of Christianity that specializes in the ordinary."[6] Pay attention, in other words, to the mundane. Honor the everyday. How inattentive we are to the fingerprints of the Almighty on the repetitious turning of the clock and calendar. How mute we believe God is, although the voice of the Lord whispers or shouts in the seeming randomness of the usual. How rich the treasure when the mentor helps the mentoree slow the pace, quiet the distractions and create space for attending to the ordinary. Questions such as the following are the tools of the mentor.

☐ Have you noticed a pattern of God's movement in your life?

☐ Did you consider what God might be saying to you in the questions you raise?

☐ What might God want you to hear in the events of your life?

Keith remembers when he broke his ankle in a volleyball game.

I thought I could still compete evenly with college students in an intramural volleyball league and did fairly well until that night when I came down on my foot wrong and heard the ankle snap. When that happened I felt the sharpest pain I had ever before experienced, but it lasted only until they put me in a cast. Then the waves of pain subsided, the sharp shooting sensation in the ankle was gone; the heightened attention to my broken body was replaced by what I considered an annoying intrusion into my schedule. What I didn't understand then was the slow process of recuperation. I resented it and initially tried to live as if I weren't carrying an eight-pound cast on my leg, until a wise friend reframed this for me saying, "Don't miss the voice of God in this time of your healing—God has your attention now while your life is only in first or second gear. Quit fighting it, and use your slow pace to listen."

God spoke to me in the very real events of my life. There was no burning bush physically aflame before my eyes, no audible voice breaking through the heavens and intoning a word to my ears, but I was given the challenge to listen to God *in the midst of my unfolding biography.*

The curriculum for the school of spiritual mentoring is the unfolding story of life as the mentoree lives it. As a good novel unfolds with unexpected twists and surprising turns of a plot, so the biography of one's life unfolds. Where it will lead is not always clear until more of the story develops. For now, it is enough to pay attention to the questions of wise and helpful mentors.

The deepest truth of spirituality is always autobiographical. It is incarnational, lived in the grit of life on Monday and Tuesday and all the days of the week. The extraordinary events of epiphany or revelation are few and rare, but the gentle or firm probing of a mentor's questions draw us back to the central action of spirituality: *to pay attention for the presence of God in everything.*

Alan Jones describes the process in unforgettable words: "My drifting is consecrated in pilgrimage."[7] The randomness of apparently disconnected drifting can become consecrated into pilgrimage through the probing of a mentor's questions. The very word *biography* comes from two words that describe the incarnational canvas of our stories: what is written *(graphia)* on our living cells *(bios).* There is a story that is being written in our lives, a composition that gets written down or painted on the canvas of our biographies. To see its image clearly, we must learn to pay attention. Spiritual mentoring is a relationship that helps us pay attention to our stories and to recognize there *the already present action of God.*

We have developed the ability for living with distraction into an accepted skill in our lives today. Our society is busy with words everywhere, many words and little hearing. Because of that, we are inattentive to holy whispers from God, and thus we doze while events of rich significance are being lived in our personal history. The gift of mentoring helps transform mere chronology into sacred story, mere biography into spiritual autobiography. Spiritual mentoring is part of the rediscovery of storytelling in the life of the soul. It seems that the church has sometimes lost its love of stories and substituted instead a love of ideas. Mentoring moves us back to "The Story" as a way to remember the stories of our own lives.

In his book on the "Story of the Christian Year" Alan Jones says,

> We need a song to sing, a story to tell, a dance to dance so that we know where we are and who we are. But we seem to have lost the art of storytelling and dreaming. Singing bits and pieces of what we know and telling snatches of half-remembered stories is better than nothing. The more we sing and tell the old, old story the less we shall be satisfied with psychological and spiritual junk food, with false and temporary means of embodiment.... There is an overall theme played in the heart of God. We have to listen to that tune and share in the larger drama if we are to make sense of our own.[8]

The mentor understands that truth is embodied in the sacred story of the individual's own biography. The Germans speak of *Heilgeschichte* as different from *Geschichte:* holy history as something much more profound than chronological history. Through the discernment of the mentor, we learn to see plot, themes, subthemes and story lines and to recognize the development of characters and of our own character. The mentor does not invent the story from disconnected pieces of story lines but rather assists the mentoree to see ever more deeply the development of the story of his or her own life. (See appendix 4, "Developing a Personal Time Line.")

Watching for the common threads in the plot of a story helped Randy challenge Clair with a deep-seated call to vocational ministry:

> Clair wanted to grab some time to chat between sessions at the retreat where I was speaking. The theme was paying attention to the importance of our stories in a mentoring relationship. Clair, a high-school teacher with several years' experience, was also a faithful elder and small-group leader in his church. His thirst for "something more" became

apparent as he began to share chapters from his own story—chapters that reflected a common theme of one whom God had called into full-time vocational ministry. In that safe space Clair was able to recognize not only the significance of his call but also the utter amazement that God was present, right there in the midst of the ordinary events of his own story.

Through the thought-provoking questions raised in mentoring, we are freed to learn to pay attention to God's presence in everything. With our days and nights we are each writing the novel of our lives, more or less aware of God, more or less attentive to the spiritual textures, more or less alive to the plot lines, more or less aware of subtle and nuanced subthemes and character development in the many chapters we write. While the Author of life started the story, we will write our own endings to our stories, with varying attention to the Author's intended plot. St. Irenaeus, bishop of Lyons (c. 130-200), writing to Christian educators, said the glory of God is a human person fully alive;[9] we take that to mean one who is aware and alert to the movement of God's presence in one's own history.

Margaret Guenther has a wonderfully frank way of speaking about the essential qualities (and hence the role) of a spiritual guide today:

> What kind of person, therefore, should be writing about the spiritual life today? She would need to be very grounded in ordinary, everyday experience. She would need to be earthy and have the ability to see the funny side of the spiritual enterprise even in the midst of great suffering. She would need to be crafty—wily enough to spot the Byzantine ploys of the ego to make itself the center of everything, even of its own suffering and struggle. She would need to be able to make judgments without being judgmental, to smell a rat without allowing her ability to discern deception to sour her vision of the glory and joy that is everyone's birthright in God.[10]

In spiritual mentoring we often begin with the most immediate, practical things of life, which ambush us into a detour back into the soul. We seldom begin with the deep experiences of spirituality but find ourselves surprised that God is lurking in that which is routine. The good mentor will help us "read between the lines" for the hidden and quietly earthy messages that God will give because life is full of God. We don't need to invent moments of God experience for people; we need to help each other see and listen and know. God is not less present to us on Monday than on Sunday! Spirituality is not something that we add on to "the real world" of jobs, family, bills and taxes; spirituality is embedded in the daily events of our biographies.

The mentor assists us to see deeply *into* and *through* the events of our lives in order to discern meaning. Have you ever wondered why God filled the Bible with stories of people and places about which we have almost no historical information? Why not streamline the pages of Scripture and publish a "one-minute Bible" that is easier and less cluttered to read? Why not eliminate the confusing names of ancient people and places? We cannot abbreviate God's story because God knew all those people and God visited all those places; God was present in their lives no less than God is present to us. God's revelation is never in a vacuum but always in geography and biography. This fact determines the course of our work in spiritual mentoring; we attend to that which God is continuously seeking to uncover in our stories.

"Spirituality requires context. Always. Boundaries, borders, limits. . . . No one becomes more spiritual by becoming less material,"[11] writes one of the most articulate of the contemporary teachers of spirituality, Eugene Peterson. Peterson was the pastor of a local congregation for nearly thirty years before moving to a position as a professor of spirituality. While he speaks primarily of pastors as spiritual directors, his words have great applicability for all spiritual mentors. Peterson understands that spiritual direction is anchored in a location. This location is the life of the mentoree and all its particulars.

"Pastoral work consists of modest, daily assigned work."[12] Peterson compares pastoral ministry to work on the farm with its routines of unglamorous chores, such as cleaning the barn, mucking out the stalls and pulling weeds. Spiritual mentoring is farm work in which we meet routinely with our mentoree for periodic unglamorous conversations and prayer. Though moments of grand epiphany burst in or around us, the heart of mentoring another is the modest work of the routine. The great hymn of the church says, "I ask no dream, no prophet ecstasy, . . . O take the dimness of my soul away." "Most pastoral work takes place in obscurity: deciphering grace in the shadows, searching out meaning in a difficult text, blowing on the embers of a hard-used life. This is hard work and not conspicuously glamorous."[13]

3. Coming Alongside: Spirituality Is Partnership with the Holy Spirit

In the book of Proverbs, Wisdom is personified in a feminine voice in a text that evokes the third foundational understanding about the nature of spiritual mentoring. In Proverbs 8:1-6 we see that Wisdom comes looking for us!

> Does not wisdom call,
> and does not understanding raise her voice?
> On the heights, beside the way,
> at the crossroads she takes her stand;
> beside the gates in front of the town,
> at the entrance of the portals she cries out:
> "To you, O people, I call,
> and my cry is to all that live.
> O simple ones, learn prudence;
> acquire intelligence, you who lack it.
> Hear, for I will speak noble things,
> and from my lips will come what is right."

Our growth does not result primarily from our efforts and commitments; instead, Wisdom takes the initiative in our direction. Wisdom comes calling! Wisdom, we discover, is God taking the initiative to seek us out, to draw us to the very throne of grace. Wisdom is God's Holy Spirit creating a partnered relationship in the work of spiritual formation.

What does it change if we understand that God initiates and we respond, that what we believe we have created is in fact our *response* to God's already active presence? It changes everything! God's heart has already felt and loved and hoped before we ever arrived. The songs of our soul have already been whispered and sung into our souls. If this notion is true, and we believe passionately that it is, then the work of the mentor is not to create but to notice, not to invent but to discern. Spiritual mentoring invites us to discover holy ground that is all around us and within, welcoming us to pay attention to the already present action of God.

In the partnership of mentoring, we are helped to pay attention to the movement of the Holy Spirit in the ordinary. Entire lives are lived without recognizing the plot that God has woven in the days and nights of time. Entire decades are lived in complete ignorance of or numbness to the fire of God's Spirit, which seeks to light the pathway with insight. It is the grand irony of "advanced" Western society that we, who look so often at ourselves, so seldom see the treasures that we are becoming through the motion of the Spirit. The mirrors used to reduce us from people into self-centered consumers have no depth that let us see the richness of our identity as the beloved of God. We are story people, people of plot, theme and character. Our lives have beginnings and middles and endings. Through mentoring we are helped to read our own lives with the delight of the novelist's audience.

Spiritual mentoring is primarily the work of the Holy Spirit. The task of helping another discover the Spirit of Christ within belongs, as Thomas Merton emphatically states, primarily to the Holy Spirit. "This is entirely a supernatural thing, for the work of rescuing the inner man from automatism belongs first to the Holy Spirit."[14]

In practical ways spiritual mentoring is the process of mentor assisting the mentoree to pay attention to the inner working of the Spirit. Spiritual mentoring is the

> curing of souls, . . . however, it is not something cleverly done by a check list of prescribed exercises, but rather by joining the action which God has already been working in the soul of the spiritual seeker. The cure of souls is a cultivated awareness that God has already seized the initiative. . . . God has been working diligently, redemptively, and strategically before I appear on the scene, before I was aware there was something here for me to do."[15]

Isaiah 48:17-18 emphasizes God's sovereign role in the work of spiritual formation:

> Thus says the LORD,
>   your Redeemer, the Holy One of Israel:
> I am the LORD your God,
>   who teaches you for your own good,
>   who leads you in the way you should go.
> O that you had paid attention to my commandments!

We call this the "already present action" of the Holy Spirit. This becomes the primary task of the mentor: *to awaken the mentoree to his or her uniqueness as a loved child of God, created in the image of God for intimacy of relationship that empowers the individual for authentic acts of ministry.* The purpose of spiritual mentoring is to create the space in which this truth is discovered. This understanding of spiritual mentoring has profoundly practical and strategic implications:

☐ Responsibility for spiritual growth is properly held in the hands of God's Holy Spirit, not in the hands of any human mentor.

☐ The initiative for spiritual growth is in the heart of God, not in the heart of the mentor.

☐ The ministry of spiritual mentoring is primarily a ministry of discernment, attention-getting and attention-giving, not of creating or forcing growth.

☐ Strategies for spiritual formation, however, may include assertive and forceful intervention in the life of the mentoree, but always with attention to the movement of God's Spirit.

Spiritual mentoring helps us discover what God desires for us and is already presently creating in the life of the mentoree through the power of the Holy Spirit. That is why we say the role of the mentor is to *facilitate* the discovery process. An appropriate analogy may be the work of the optometrist, whose task is simply to adjust the intensity of light through a series of lenses in order for the patient to have better vision. The optometrist does not invent the light or create the patient's eyes; rather he or she helps focus the patient's attention on the light that is already present. The relationship of spiritual mentoring is three-dimensional and dynamic: mentor and Holy Spirit, mentor and mentoree, mentoree and Holy Spirit. Attentive listening, attentive prayer and active discernment are necessary in all three essential relationships, by all three participants. To come alongside is to participate in partnership with the Holy Spirit in the work of ministry.

The person who has been guided by the effective use of spiritual mentoring understands that the discovery of the already present action of the Spirit is brought about by an attitude and life of prayer. Most narrowly defined, spiritual direction is direction offered in the prayer life of the individual Christian. But in a broader sense, it is an art that includes helping to discern the movements of the Holy Spirit in all of our lives, assisting us to become obedient to these movements and offering support in the crucial life decisions that our faithfulness requires. Prayer, thus understood, embraces all of life, and spiritual direction is therefore an essential ministerial task.[16]

A young priest who took the name John of the Cross sought out Teresa of Ávila to be his mentor. He was not the only one mentored by Teresa, but the story of their spiritual relationship is fascinating because in time John of the Cross would become her mentor. What made Teresa of Ávila attractive as a mentor for John of the Cross we are not told in their stories, but it is clear that many others also wished to learn from her how to deepen their love for Jesus. Her thoughts about her writing, however, may give us profound insights in our conversation about qualifications for mentors. Her books were written out of obedience, at the command of her superiors in the convent in which she served, not out of a sense of her own giftedness as a writer or her competence as a thinker or spiritual director.

She once exclaimed,

> For the love of God, let me work at my spinning wheel and to the choir and perform the duties of the religious life, like the other sisters. I am not meant to write: I have neither the health nor the intelligence for it.
>
> The authority of persons so learned and serious as my confessors suffices for the approval of any good thing I may say, if the Lord gives me grace to say it, in which case it will not be mine but His; for I have no learning, nor have I led a good life, nor do I get my information from a learned man or from any other person whatsoever. Only those who have commanded me to write this know that I am doing so, and at the moment they are not here. I am almost stealing time for writing and that with great difficulty, for it hinders me from spinning and I am living in a poor house and have numerous things to do.[17]

These words of humility were written by a woman whose words have now been read and reread by millions, a woman whose works have now been translated into dozens of other languages, the author of one of the most widely read books ever written by a Spanish author. Her work was the work of her heart and her personal, mystical experience with her God rather than the work of a serious or systematic academician. Her humility endears her to all who read her work, and her honesty of expression appeals to all as well. She became a mentor to millions, though she didn't believe she had the competence of her learned superiors. She illustrates poignantly that such humility of heart is essential for anyone who wishes to be an effective mentor. The mentor sees herself as partner in something much larger than her own creativity or wisdom.

4. The Trajectory of Spiritual Formation: Spiritual Mentoring Is Purposive
An interesting book on travel as pilgrimage defines pilgrimage in much the
same way we have talked about spiritual mentoring:

> *Pilgrimage* is the kind of journeying that marks just this move from
> mindless to mindful, soulless to soulful travel. The difference may be
> subtle or dramatic; by definition it is life-changing. It means being alert
> to the times when all that's needed is a trip to a remote place to simply
> *lose* yourself, and to the times when what's needed is a journey to a
> sacred place, in all its glorious and fearsome masks, to *find* yourself.[18]

Mentoring has a trajectory, an aim, a target and a purpose. It is not
mindless or soulless meandering but a journey that recognizes itself as
pilgrimage, a journey with a spiritual or devotional purpose. The trajectory is
purposive but not prepackaged. Our spiritual journeys are not given to us
complete with road map, trip outline or itinerary, only an invitation to discover
what God has in mind for our particular excursion through time and space.

It is the task of the mentor to help us sink deep enough into our lives to
discover that purpose. A brief look at some biblical mentors will allow us to
construct a partial list of mentoring purposes.

Encouragement. Moses tells young Joshua, his successor in leadership, to
be strong and not to fear what lies ahead. Deuteronomy 31:7-8 powerfully
illustrates the encouraging role of a mentor.

Discernment. The old priest Eli instructed his young servant, Samuel, to
listen. First Samuel 3:8 tells us that after several experiences, "Eli perceived
that the LORD was calling the boy" and helped his young mentoree to a deep
level of discernment through listening.

Accountability. The prophet Nathan confronts King David for his moral
failures in his adulterous affair and abuse of power to force Bathsheba, a
married woman, to have sex with him. Second Samuel 12 is a text of
confrontation and accountability.

A reminder of spiritual identity. The fascinating story of Abigail tells of a
young woman who intercepts the young political refugee David when he has
lost his godly focus and is about to take revenge on her husband, a wealthy
landowner named Nabal. She intervenes in a wonderfully creative way to
bring to David's mind the memory of his God-given purposes. She cannot
confront or challenge the raging and angry young soldier, David, but she can

use her wits and her beauty to gently restore David's memory of God's purpose for his life (1 Samuel 25).

Wisdom-giving for decision-making. In the wonderful story of a biblical friendship, Naomi is the wise sage for young Ruth, who carefully follows the instructions of the older woman for decisions about her young life.

Challenge for political influence. Mordecai challenges his young niece, the queen Esther, to remember her identity as one of the people of God (Esther 4).

Empowerment. One of the most interesting mentoring relationships is that of Elijah, the elder prophet and teacher of his school of young prophets, who empowers Elisha, the prophet who will become his successor. In 2 Kings 2, Elisha asks for a double portion of the power that Elijah possesses.

Explanation and correction. Priscilla and Aquila are a married couple who have no apparent theological education other than their own experience of the heart. Nonetheless, they tutor the great preacher and teacher of their day, Apollos. In Acts 18 we have a wonderful text that shows the role of the laity in teaching those who teach.

Appeal for growth. Paul writes to his friend Philemon, appealing for a fundamental shift in worldview that will result in a dramatic change in Philemon's relationship with his runaway slave, Onesimus. The story of Paul's newest protégé, his "son in the faith," the slave Onesimus, illustrates the power of the gospel to fashion a new model for relationships. Paul addresses the issue of slavery by addressing the very particular, local and personal issue of a runaway slave and his reentry into the household of the wealthy master, Philemon. The church spoke a challenge to slavery then even as it challenges racism or classism today.

Having seen that spiritual mentoring can fulfill these many purposes, one should realize that there are many purposes that spiritual mentoring does not fulfill. Spiritual mentoring is *not*

☐ career counseling, though it may ask the questions of vocation and call
☐ psychological counseling, though it may probe the life of the inward psyche of another
☐ advice-giving, though wisdom is the language spoken by mentors
☐ pastoral counseling, though it may be practiced by those pastors gifted for mentoring
☐ teaching in a traditional meaning of transmitting information, though it will include times of instruction

☐ discipling, where the goal is to teach a believer foundational truths and personal mastery of spiritual disciplines

☐ confession of one to another, though the mentor may assist the spiritual seeker to give voice to his or her own confession to God

Nine values of spiritual mentoring have emerged from our study of the historic and classical writings on spiritual direction. We will further develop these values throughout the book, but we want to list them here to emphasize the very practical purposes of the work of spiritual mentoring. Spiritual mentoring

☐ provides an effective means of enhancing intimacy with God

☐ cultivates recognition of the already present action of God in the life of the mentoree through the Holy Spirit

☐ aids in the discernment of God's will

☐ is a highly effective means for character and value formation

☐ facilitates ultimate identity discovered as a loved and accept child of God

☐ is a necessity for the journey of faith

☐ provides clarity and guidance for decisions and service for one's life

☐ is a source of encouragement, courage and hope

☐ is rooted in the teaching of the church and biblical truth

5. The Essential Art: Spiritual Mentoring Requires Listening

Spiritual mentoring is a ministry of paraclete (lowercase *p*) in partnership with the ministry of Paraclete (uppercase *P*), that is, the ministry of one who "comes alongside" to empower, listen, love and illumine just as the Holy Spirit comes alongside as the Paraclete. *Paraclete* is the Greek term often used of an attorney who "comes alongside" a client in the courtroom. The spiritual mentor is one who comes alongside another for a period of time, brief or extended, in partnership with the Holy Spirit, for the explicit task of nurturing spiritual formation in the life of the mentoree. The one who comes alongside is not necessarily one who has been evaluated, trained and certified for the technical work of spiritual mentoring but is rather one capable of listening, loving, empowering and shining light on the life of the mentoree.

Spiritual mentoring is not primarily the work of creating something, doing something, causing growth or any of the other activities so often connected with ministry. It is rather the ministry of participating in what God is already doing in the life of the mentoree. This character defines the nature of spiritual mentoring as a work of sensitive listening and coming alongside another with an open heart.

The heart of mentoring is the attentive, discerning mentor who, sometimes intuitively, knows how to listen to the Spirit of God. When I am listened to, probed, encouraged, challenged and helped to hear God's voice, then the mentor has come alongside. When mentoring becomes reduced to techniques and systems, then the spirituality of mentoring is in danger. Spiritual mentoring is any of the ways we "come alongside" to assist another to listen to God and to discover the already present action of God in that person's life.

"You cannot give away what you don't have" is a simple summary of the absolute precondition for any spiritual guide or mentor: you cannot give to others what is lacking in yourself. This statement breeds fear and feelings of inadequacy in some: "I cannot even pretend to be a mentor to others, then, because I never seem to have it all figured out for myself." Most of us sense our own weaknesses and ineptitude in the development of our own spirituality. We know that we have not yet attained full spirituality, but we "press on toward the mark" as Paul encourages us to do. Others may deny their need for further growth and say, instead, "I *can* be a mentor because I have already been through so many of the 'stages' of spiritual growth."

These can be destructive attitudes because they misunderstand the purpose and process of spiritual mentoring—they assume the mentor's task is to do something for the other person by teaching, correcting or otherwise giving something the mentor possesses, something the mentoree lacks. No. A spiritual mentor must be a listener—to God first, to self second and to the mentoree third or to all three simultaneously. The task of the spiritual mentor to create a space for learning requires that the mentor have a spirit of teachableness. When we believe that we must be competent in all things or nearly so, we misunderstand the primary qualities necessary for the spiritual mentor.

Who have been the most effective teachers in your life, in the classroom and outside? Have they not been those people whose lives were passionately in love with something about which they knew and about which you longed to learn more? Think of that biology teacher or professor who lived for the study of microbes, the carpenter whose life rang with a passionate love for working in wood, the mother whose love for nurturing her children fulfilled her life. If they were good teachers of their own loves, they created a space for others to learn *from* them and *with* them. The gospel is the song that unites us all. As we tell others of our own passionate song, we free others to sing out their song as well. In the singing of our songs, there is a connection to something that is grand, the opus of God's own Story in the world.

Many of the great educational philosophers throughout history have understood that teaching and learning are not discrete activities but belong together. An ancient way of speaking about the church described the church as *ecclesia docens semper ecclesia dicens*, which translates as "the teaching church is always the learning church." This leads us to the concept of "educator as leading learning."[19] The mentor who will be a wise voice for others is always the mentor whose own ear is turned toward the wisdom of others, an ear that is open to listen, to hear and to transform life. The mentor serves best who remains the number-one learner.

"Guides who are going to reach spiritually awakening women and men in our times must be awake themselves. A guide who has lost her or his experiential connection with the Mystery will not long be credible. Guides must be people who are moved by the 'dynamics of delight.' They must be faithful to the inviting joy of that encounter. And they must be willing to share that delight with others."[20] They have learned such attention through their own active lives of listening.

The autobiography of Therese of Lisieux, *Story of a Soul,* is a poignant story of a deep and loving relationship with Jesus. Therese came to see that Christian living wasn't about knowing what needs to be done, but about doing it. She wrote, "As little birds learn to sing by listening to their parents, so children learn the science of virtue, the sublime song of Divine Love from souls responsible for forming them."[21] The mentor who is listening to God and others invites the mentoree to join in listening to that concert of God's music.

6. One Size Does Not Fit All: Spiritual Mentoring Requires Adaptable Discernment

John of the Cross said that spiritual directors should be able to see the way "by which God is leading the soul, and if they know it not, let them leave the soul in peace and not disturb it."[22] The importance of the spiritual gift of discernment cannot be overstated. Discernment is the ability to see deeply into the truth of a person's life or situation. To discern is to see wisely. There are many who can see analytically or critically, but rare are those with the spirit of discernment. The sixth foundation for spiritual mentoring is adaptable discernment.

Discernment asks questions like the following: What is God up to in this situation? Where is God's hand at work in this? What is the sacred text to be read in the sacred moment before us? What might these ordinary moments contain of the God dimension? The mentor with a discerning eye is one who sees more than the mere recital of facts, chronologies and events. To discern is to see with the vision of God. In 1 Thessalonians 5:21, Paul speaks of the essential skill of discernment: "but test everything; hold fast to what is good."

Before we can hold fast, we must assess. First John also calls us to discern the spirits, to test, to seek the wise pathway. In *The Message* Eugene Peterson translates the first several verses of 1 John 4 as follows:

> My dear friends, don't believe everything you hear. Carefully weigh and examine what people tell you. Not everyone who talks about God comes from God. There are a lot of lying preachers loose in the world. Here's how you test for the genuine Spirit of God. Everyone who confesses openly his faith in Jesus Christ—the Son of God, who came as an actual flesh-and-blood person—comes from God and belongs to God. And everyone who refuses to confess faith in Jesus has nothing in common with God.

In 1 Corinthians 12:4-11 Paul says there are various gifts, one of which is the gift of discernment or recognizing spirits. Though one can be trained to listen with discernment, there is a gift of discernment that comes only from a life lived walking close to God. It is the exercise of sharply tuned ears, focused eyes, an attentive heart. Such a one has a disposition for seeking the wisdom of Proverbs 3:5-8, which says,

> Trust in the LORD with all your heart,
>   and do not rely on your own insight.
> In all your ways acknowledge him,
>   and he will make straight your paths.
> Do not be wise in your own eyes;
>   fear the LORD, and turn away from evil.
> It will be a healing for your flesh
>   and a refreshment for your body.

A young college student came to the campus ministry office with a deep spiritual concern. Born an "MK," a missionary kid, she had "practiced" Christian faith more than she ever sang the music in her own voice, and now she found her prayers to be lifeless, without joy or meaning. Her spirituality was anemic; her prayer life was a trivialized exercise in meaninglessness. We sat together in a spirit of waiting on the Lord, and finally I proposed a daring thought. "Stop praying!" The words were spoken to her with increasing confidence. "Stop praying! Can you do that? Don't pray again until you need to."

She agreed with some uncertainty, and silently a prayer was raised for her well-being in the days ahead. Within a few days, less than a week to be exact, she was back with a glow of light in her eyes. "I only lasted a few days, and then I couldn't hold out any longer. I prayed because I wanted to, because I needed to, and it is a rich time for me now."

Discernment came with a bold, apparently crazy spiritual intuition: "Stop praying!" Who suggests that as a method of spiritual growth? But there proved to be something of wisdom in those words that emerged from a prayerful and listening heart.

Another discouraged young student was sent out with the assignment to read Ephesians 1 every day for a month. When she returned, she said, "I wasn't sure about why I should keep reading those words over and over again, but eventually they felt familiar and I realized something. I have never felt so loved by anyone as I did morning by morning because I realized that God planned for me long before I arrived."

> Blessed be the God and Father of our Lord Jesus Christ, who has blessed us in Christ with every spiritual blessing in the heavenly places, just as he chose us in Christ before the foundation of the world to be holy and blameless before him in love. (Eph 1:3-4)

There is an individuality to the work of spiritual mentoring that cannot be ignored. There are not simple formulae or steps to be followed in every case; certainly no recipes list the five steps every mentoree should take for spiritual growth. Perhaps Ignatius of Loyola summarizes best the mindset of adaptive discernment for the mentor when he says,

> He who gives the Exercises should not turn or incline himself to one side or the other, but keeping in the middle like a balance, should allow the Creator to work immediately with the creature, and the creature with its Creator and Lord.[23]

The mentoree brings raw materials to the mentoring relationship—questions, issues, struggles, ideas, hopes, dreams, information, misinformation—the basic stuff of life. No two mentors are likely to do exactly the same thing with a mentoree in each situation. The goal is not to copy some perfect plan created by another but rather to discern wise pathways for the particular mentoree. There is not likely going to be a "right" pathway in every case; more likely a multitude of options will emerge, requiring adaptation and discernment.

7. Not Only for Specialists: Spiritual Mentoring Belongs to the Priesthood of All Believers

The ancient work of spiritual direction was, in many cases, the specialist's role, even as it is today. It was often a highly structured, hierarchical relationship with a one-way focus—eyes trained on the spiritual formation of the spiritual seeker alone. We would argue, however, that spiritual mentoring has become a ministry for the entire priesthood of believers, something to be practiced at kitchen tables, in offices, laboratories, factories and warehouses, on assembly-lines, on buses and in car-pools, as well as in Sunday-school classrooms and churches, for everywhere there are wise mentors and those ready to be mentored. A brief glance back at biblical mentors supports this well. Eunice for Timothy, Philemon for Paul, Abigail for David, Aquila and Priscilla for the great theology teacher Apollos, and Uncle Mordecai for his young niece Esther—all of these people possessed the heart of the mentor, though few could have hung out their shingle for an official, "licensed" practice of mentoring. The integrity of their lives authorized them for ministries of spiritual guidance. Spiritual mentoring fits the present mode of life in the church because of its informality, diversity of style and mutuality.

Mentors come in all sizes and shapes, all backgrounds and training, all abilities and styles, all races and economic positions, male and female, young and old. It is the wonder of God's creativity that each person's experience is unique and uniquely valuable—all are different though all share the mark of God's stamp. God honored each of us in creating us at our birth, and God continues to honor us by inviting us to be agents of reconciliation and ambassadors of divine love, grace and hope. Mentoring belongs to the whole body of Christ as we seek together to listen to God, the Holy Spirit, who comes alongside as Paraclete, often through the life of the mentor-paraclete. Even a cursory survey of biblical characters reveals a variety of backgrounds, relationships and purposes for mentoring. Biblical mentors were not of a single class, gender, background or history; they represented people from many backgrounds who intervened in people's lives for many different purposes.

Some have argued that "Anyone can / Everyone should,"[24] and some have argued the opposite, that "anyone can mentor, but not everyone should."[25] Certainly, anyone can mentor another in a skill, interest or experience in which they are especially competent. Age may be a factor that qualifies one for such mentoring; experience with a topic, organization or activity may be another. Spiritual mentoring, however, is not as simple as telling someone else about your experiences or proclaiming your ideas; it requires a highly developed ability for listening and discerning. One definition of the word says that to mentor is to hold up a mirror for reflection. What is reflected is what inhabits the life of the mentoree, not the brilliance of the mentor.

We conclude that spiritual mentoring does not belong only in the hands of the specialists. While some may be especially gifted for mentoring, spiritual mentoring is the work of the community of faith just as friendship belongs to all people. We wish to assist in a revolution to return the ministry of spiritual mentoring to the community of faith itself. Numerous exhortations to biblical practices as community contribute to this understanding of the priesthood of believers, for example, "urge one another to good works," "speak truth in love," "confess to one another," "pray for one another." Who, therefore, is capable of such a ministry? We believe it belongs in the wise hearts, listening ears and alert minds of the larger body of Christ. Some of the classical writers even suggest that spiritual direction is not something one seeks to do; mentorees come seeking a mentor.

The skills of mentors can be developed and need to be enhanced in the life of anyone called to this ministry. To limit the ministry of mentoring to clergy alone will continue to impoverish the spirituality of the church. If the hospitality of spiritual friendship is a provocative image for understanding spiritual mentoring, which we believe it is, then the questions of proficiency for the task become transformed. No longer are the issues matters of office, formal education or ecclesiastical licensure; they are issues of readiness and capability: Are you spiritually prepared to help others become friends with you and with God? Are you capable of nurturing friendship and hospitality? Are you sensitive to the whisper of God in your own life and able to assist another to listen for the sometimes gentle chords of God's song in them? Then you have some of the necessary prerequisites for the ministry of spiritual mentoring.

Eugene Peterson tells the story of his encounter with his first spiritual mentor. The man was a member of the church in Montana where Peterson grew up. Peterson, at age twenty, home from college for the summer and anxious for spiritual conversation, was guided to meet with the fix-it man, a jack-of-all-trades in their town, Reuben Lance.

> My first spiritual director didn't know he was a spiritual director. He had never so much as heard the term spiritual director, and neither had I. But our mutual ignorance of terminology did not prevent the work. We were both doing something for which we had no name. For a summer of Tuesday and Thursday evenings we met, conversing and praying in the prayer room in the church basement. We got on well. He was not only the first but among the best of the spiritual directors I have had. . . . It was accomplished by means of Reuben's prayerful listening. He had nothing to tell me, although he freely talked about himself when it was appropriate. But he never took over.[26]

According to Peterson, there were only two skills or preconditions necessary for the mentoring that Reuben Lance provided so unself-consciously and so well: unknowing and uncaring. *Unknowing* refers to the moments when "diligent catechesis is not required and a "leisurely pause before mystery is."[27] *Uncaring* refers to the detachment of heart and spirit when the mentor gets out of the way and allows the Holy Spirit to do the caring. As Peterson points out, "There are moments when caring is not required, when detachment is appropriate. What the Spirit is doing in other persons far exceeds what we ourselves are doing."[28]

Such wisdom is certainly hard to acquire through formal education in the Western world. We are taught to know, and we are motivated to care. Such activities animate us and validate us in the work of ministry for others. The wisdom of Peterson's experience is the paradox of knowing and caring enough not to interfere. Ordination or a degree is not a prerequisite for such skills.

For Reflection

What then are the necessary requisites for the one who would be mentor? Ask yourself:

☐ What "wisdom" do you most need from another?

☐ What character do you seek in a spiritual friend?

☐ What moves you toward another person who might become your spiritual guide?

Characteristics of a Mentor

Teachers are assessed and certified; schools are evaluated according to their successes in teaching; as a society we believe we can determine what makes a good or a bad teacher. There are measures and ways to evaluate and answer the question, What is a teacher? Even coaches are rated for their skill, productivity and success. What about the spiritual mentor? Is there a set of tools to help us evaluate or measure the potential capabilities in a spiritual mentor? In the human resources industry, people are evaluated every day on whether they "have what it takes" to be effective in their various jobs. How can we discern the readiness, ability or potential in one asked to become a spiritual mentor? Athletic scouts and coaches study the talent and potential for players in their sports, always alert to discern: Do they have what it takes? Can they be what they set out to be in their chosen arena of competition? In this chapter we have suggested foundational "scouting" questions: Who can dare assume the lofty role of spiritual mentor for another? Are there measures that can help one assess a person's readiness, ability or competence as a mentor? When all is said and done, after all, What is a mentor?

We don't believe there are tests that easily assess or evaluations that easily measure one's competence in mentoring, as if this art form were a scientific or objective science to which hard research or quantitative analysis might apply. We believe instead that there are markings that suggest some of the essential skills and qualities common to spiritual mentors:

☐ a role model worthy of emulation

☐ a life of holiness, spiritual maturity, biblical knowledge and wisdom

☐ someone who practices a life of spiritual disciplines, including prayer

☐ one skilled in the hard labor of attentive, reflective listening

☐ one gifted in recognizing potential in people

☐ one gifted in spiritual discernment of God's already present action

☐ someone who has an ability to foster an atmosphere of trust, acceptance and space

☐ one who is experienced in life

☐ one who can create "disciplines of grace," accountability with the mentoree

Five Dynamics of Spiritual Mentoring

In order to better understand the mentoring processes, a discussion of five guiding dynamics first identified by J. Robert Clinton will form a framework within which to accomplish spiritual mentoring. These will be the topics for discussion in the following chapters. We do not understand mentoring as following a mechanical progression or imposed program through these five stages, but we see them as an organic, natural interaction of processes in the community established between mentor and mentoree.

☐ Attraction: initiating and establishing the mentoring relationship, which includes the phase of attraction

☐ Relationship: nurturing a hospitable relationship of trust and intimacy

☐ Responsiveness: sustaining the dynamic of teachability through development of responsiveness in the mentoree

☐ Accountability: refining growth in the mentoree through specific disciplines of accountability

☐ Empowerment: releasing the mentoree for continued growth through an empowered awareness of intimacy with God, identity as a child of God and a unique voice for kingdom responsibility

Further Reflection for the Mentor

1. With which style of mentoring are you most familiar?

2. About which style of spiritual mentoring are you most curious?

3. As you think about the list of biblical mentors and the various purposes of their relationship with others, which one are you most likely to desire in your own mentoring relationship?

4. Review the seven "essentials" of spiritual mentoring described in this chapter and reflect further on the importance of each one for the task of spiritual mentoring.

5. How will you seek to develop and notice the partnership with the Holy Spirit as you mentor another person?

Further Reflection for the Mentoree

1. Remember once again people who have been your mentors in life. What roles did they play in your life?

2. Do you have any experience in sharing your autobiography with another person? To whom have you told your story or selected "chapters"? (See appendix 4, "Developing a Personal Time Line.")

3. Which style of mentoring is familiar or most comfortable for you?

4. Review the seven essentials of spiritual mentoring described in this chapter and reflect further on the importance of each one for your life as a mentoree.

5. How can you as a partner in the process of spiritual mentoring help your mentor notice your relationship with the Holy Spirit?

Three

The Art of Beginning Well
Attraction

Be what you would have your pupils to be.
THOMAS CARLYLE

I n the winter of 1118 Bernard of Clairvaux was a sick man, weakened by
fasting and overwork, living in austerity and simplicity in a crude cottage.
One of his young students, William of St.-Thierry, visited that primitive
hut and described his response to the man he found there.

> In that hut, like the shelters assigned to the lepers at the crossroads, I
> found him radiant with joy, as though he had been caught up in the
> delights of paradise. Bending my gaze upon the kingly dwelling and its
> inhabitant, I was filled with such awe—God is my witness—as though
> I had drawn near the altar of God. I conceived of such a fondness for
> the man that I longed to share the poverty and the simplicity of his life.
> Had I then been granted one wish, it would have been to stay with him
> forever, as his servant.

Seventeen years later William became a Cistercian. His life was changed
forever because of his encounter with a man who would become his mentor.
It started, quite unintentionally, in a moment of spiritual attraction that
caused William to long "to share the poverty and simplicity of his life."[1]

What we call *attraction* is the phase of initiating and establishing the
relationship for mentoring. We may not have the dramatic encounter with
another that William had, and we may not be as movingly stirred by the life

we see, but we will experience a movement of God's Spirit within that causes attraction to the heart or spirit or life of another. Attraction is the basic human response of curiosity, interest and appeal. It begins when you notice the integrity, skill or other attributes of someone whom you respect. It begins when you wonder if this person before you may know something about the spiritual journey that will help you take the next steps you long to take. Something in the other person engages your interest and draws you to that person as a potential mentor.

Potential mentors may not be leaders who do their work in highly visible ways or with the spotlight constantly shining on them. They may be quiet, unobtrusive people to whom you are attracted as people of character. In fact, the best mentors are often the people whom you may overlook or bypass because they have no official office or role in ministry. Attraction begins the more intentional mentoring relationship and starts the conversation between two people. There is, in other words, a time when one recognizes in another a quality, a faith, a spirit, something that compels or attracts and thus creates a motivation to learn from the other.[2]

In this chapter we will focus on the question, How do you "begin well" in a spiritual mentoring relationship? How do you enter a relationship with someone to whom you are drawn for help in spiritual development? Who takes the initiative—the mentor or the mentoree? What are essential foundational steps that will anchor the relationship? Are there healthy boundaries to establish for the relationship? In this chapter we will talk about the necessary steps in initiating a relationship for mentoring and will offer a practical format for creating a covenant between mentor and mentoree.

Initiating the Relationship

Ken was at a crossroads, needing someone to listen to his tangled life and help him make sense of it spiritually. Steve was someone whom Ken respected greatly as a man of God who was "tuned in" to the movement of the Spirit. If anyone could provide spiritual direction for Ken, it was Steve. After all, Steve was highly educated in the Christian classics, taught courses in spiritual formation and regularly took seminary students to the Black Hills of South Dakota for a course entitled Wilderness Theology.

As his academic adviser, Randy had encouraged Ken to seek out someone to whom he was attracted who could help him discover the already present action of God in the midst of his rather complex life issues. Ken considered asking Steve but was hesitant because he thought it would not be the proper way to go about starting a mentoring relationship. Asking someone to mentor him seemed rather odd. Ken's response was typical: "Shouldn't the mentor ask the mentoree to strike up a mentoring relationship?"

Ken's question reflects one of the most common questions related to mentoring: Is it okay if I ask someone to mentor me? The unfortunate truth of the matter is that people who desire a spiritual mentoring relationship will wait a long time if they wait on the initiative of a spiritual mentor to whom they are attracted. More often than not spiritual mentors are sought out by potential mentorees.

Two contemporary students in the field of spiritual direction, Marie Theresa Coombs and Francis Kelly Nemeck, argue that the initiation process has mostly landed in the hands of the mentoree. In fact, they strongly believe one of the primary ways people know they have the "charism" of spiritual direction is if they are sought out for spiritual guidance. "Thus, a basic sign of a call to become a spiritual director resides in the fact that one is sought out by others for spiritual direction."[3]

Jon was aggressive in seeking out mentoring. He walked into the office and stated his case: "I believe I can be helped by learning from you, and I'd like to come to you regularly (weekly) for mentoring conversations." The stage of attraction had been there for some time, and he acted on his heart impulses.

Peter, on the other hand, is reserved and needed the mentor to seek him out with similar words: "Peter, I believe that you have great potential for leadership, and I'd like you to consider entering a mentoring relationship with me."

Whether the mentoree seeks out a mentor or the mentor does the seeking, a spiritual mentoring relationship begins by paying attention to another. There is a "chemistry" to this initial moment in the mentoring relationship; an attraction occurs. How it begins varies widely. Sometimes the "attraction" for mentor and mentoree is rational and easily explained—there is already a working relationship, or both are part of a small-group study, or one is a teacher and the other a student. At other times it appears to be an oddly serendipitous experience—how the two find each other is often a surprising gift of God. However it may happen, attraction refers to the first stage, an experience of noticing another and finding yourself interested in what that person can offer you as a possible spiritual mentor. Attraction is stage one, but it is only the beginning. We return to one of our historic mentors as an example of the early stages in the mentoring work.

Attract Them by Your Way of Life

Augustine was born in A.D. 354 in Tagaste, a small North African town, in what is present-day Algeria. He arrived on the scene of Christian history some forty years after Constantine became the first Christian Roman Emperor. Augustine's mother, Monica, was more than a faithful follower of Christ; she passionately loved and served her God. There is no record of his father's ever being known as a believer. It was Monica who played a significant role in her son's spiritually formative years and who offered many prayers for her son's salvation and service to God.

At the age of seventeen Augustine left home to begin his formal education in Carthage in the study of rhetoric. In those years of young adulthood, he succumbed to sexual promiscuity and fathered a son while living with his mistress. But during his academic pursuit he came to a crucial spiritual turning point. Upon hearing the rhetorical skill and rather academic presentation of the gospel by Bishop Ambrose, "Augustine was impressed by what he considered a perfectly acceptable academic approach to literature. He then began to reconsider his earlier views about Christianity."[4]

Shortly thereafter, at a friend's garden in 386 he found he could no longer run from the beating conviction in his heart, and he surrendered his life to the love of God. In an often repeated story, Augustine tells of an encounter that was to change his life forever. While he sat amid the serene beauty of the formal garden, he heard a voice repeat several times, "Take and read. Take and read." He looked around and saw no one but later believed the voice was sent from God to motivate his own study of Scripture. He sat there wrestling within himself about his life, faith and spirituality until those words caused him to "take up and read" the Bible. Through that study he repented of his profligate life and turned to become a follower of Jesus Christ. He left his mistress and returned with his son to North Africa to pursue the monastic life. In 396 he became a bishop, replacing Valerius of Hippo. His famous *Confessions* tell his story in honest narrative, revealing his flawed humanity for all to see.

Augustine's own words challenge us in the early phase of attraction. He wrote with what seems to be a tone of cynicism or at least a word of caution for those who spend their time in academic study without the accompanying practice of spirituality and faith. His intention, however, was to challenge the young student to learn with life and heart, as well as intellect. The document called *To Diocorus, a Student* is Augustine's reply to the myriad questions raised by young Diocorus. His essay trumpets the essential cry of attraction: "Attract them by your way of life." Just as it is axiomatic that "the heart of Christian education is the heart of the Christian educator," so the heart of spiritual mentoring is the heart (character) of the spiritual mentor as the Holy Spirit is present in the heart of the mentor.

> Finally, suppose that, when you've been asked all the questions you've sent to me, you've been able to respond. Lo, people now call you supremely learned and acute! Lo, Greek breath lifts you to heaven on its praises! But remember your own worth, and your reason for wanting to deserve this praise: to teach something supremely important and wholesome to the people you have so easily impressed with your trifling talk, and who are now hanging onto your words with such eagerness and goodwill.
>
> What I would like to know is whether you possess and can accurately impart to others anything supremely important and wholesome. It's ridiculous, if, after you've learned a lot of unnecessary things in order to prepare people to listen to you tell that what is indispensable, you yourself don't possess it; and if, while you are busy learning how to get their attention, you refuse to learn what to teach them when you've gained it. But if you say that you already know, and answer that it's Christian doctrine (I hope that you prefer this to everything else and entrust your hope of eternal salvation to this alone), you don't need to be familiar with the dialogues of Cicero and a collection of the beggarly and divided opinions of other people to win an audience. *Attract them by your way of life if you want them to receive such a teaching from you.*[5]

The last sentence in the quotation from Augustine contains volumes of information about the early stages in the process of mentoring. "Attract them by your way of life" means that integrity of life is primary. Augustine did not live a perfect life as a man of faith, but there was an honesty in his famous *Confessions* that provides an insight into the attraction of character or the attraction of a life of integrity. To know the words is important. To sing the song is an altogether different thing! It is frequently said of Augustine that in the honesty of his own spiritual pilgrimage in his *Confessions* many hear echoes of their own stories of the spiritual journey. His public and brutally honest personal confessions were unheard of during his time, especially in written communication. Some even suggest that *The Confessions* serve as a precursor for the personal spiritual journal that many have found to be an indispensable discipline for their own spiritual formation.

Although he did not primarily write from a spiritual mentoring perspective, his personal faith story gives strong suggestion of the value he placed in its purpose in his own spiritual formation process. His faith was mentored by those spiritual directors he knew as his "confessors," those who listened, absolved his sin and empowered him for the pilgrimage. One need not agree with all of his theology or practice to recognize the historical significance of this early Christian thinker. His views and treatment of women are problematic for many today. He was not a man whose life consistently and evenly modeled the best of Christian character and behavior, but perhaps that is what authorizes him best as worthy of our attention. If Augustine's story, as messy, flawed, imperfect and sometimes misguided as it was, reflected a life used by God to influence many others, perhaps our own less-than-perfect lives can also be used for the spiritual development of others on their journey of life.

The extravagant boldness of an Augustine is a supreme example of this transformation. This same man who wrote his *Confessions* for all the world to read boldly says later, "Attract them by your way of life." Hypocrite? Rogue? Fool? Or one transformed by grace and thus freed to learn from his monumental failures and willing to use his own flaws as the curriculum for the faith formation of others. Starting well begins not with attention on the mentoree but with attention by the would-be mentor to his or her own life and to the honesty of his or her own story.

Augustine held a high regard for the integrity of relationships he found with those whom he considered his confessors. His understanding of this relationship was not one in which he sought out others for the sole purpose of the confession of his sins, but rather one that was necessary for the Christian journey. Augustine believed that these individuals were appointed in a timely manner by God for the primary purpose of providing guidance in order for the mentoree to live a life of holiness and service. Real people telling real stories of real life—that's the essence of spiritual mentoring.

Why then are we so afraid to fully embrace every twist and turn of our stories? A significant truth of the gospel is that our stories are uniquely given to us, in order to help others recognize the value and uniqueness of their own stories. In order to begin well in our spiritual mentoring relationships, we must first have the courage to honor our own stories. We must recognize that God has made each of us a worthy character.

For Reflection
☐ When was the last time your story was heard by others?
☐ When was the last time you celebrated the powerful uniqueness of your life? How?
☐ When was the last time you were gripped by your weaknesses?
☐ Can you see your weaknesses, flaws and failures as necessary for character development?

The Stories of Our Lives
Embracing one's story is not an easy task. Perhaps Eugene Peterson is correct in suggesting that our way of reading the biblical stories distorts our reading of the stories of our own lives.

> The reason that story is so basic to us is that life itself has a narrative shape—a beginning and end, plot and characters, conflict and resolution. Life isn't an accumulation of abstractions such as love and truth, sin and salvation, atonement and holiness; life is the realization of details that all connect organically, personally, specifically: names and fingerprints, street numbers and local weather, lamb for supper and a flat tire in the rain. God reveals himself to us not in a metaphysical formulation or a cosmic fireworks display but in the kind of stories that we use to tell our children who they are and how to grow up as human beings, tell our friends who we are and what it's like to be human. . . . Somewhere along the way, most of us pick up bad habits of extracting from the Bible what we pretentiously call "spiritual principles" or "moral guidelines," or "theological truths," and then corseting ourselves in them in order to force a godly shape on our lives.[6]

Have we been trying hard to measure up to the "principles" we have created from Scripture, rather than embrace and celebrate our blemished, embarrassing, scarred lives for the stories of redeemed grace they are? Like Augustine, we too can live a life worthy of emulation—worthy of the attraction of others on the journey of faith. The process begins with accepting our own stories, with accepting ourselves for who we are and where we are in our own journey, complete with defects, embarrassments, disappointments and fears. It is here we can claim the truth the Corinthians were urged to embrace from Paul's story of weakness and the power of the resurrection that shone through it, " 'for power is made perfect in weakness.' So, I will boast all the more gladly of my weaknesses, so that the power of Christ may dwell in me" (2 Cor 12:9).

Jaquie was in Randy's spiritual development group at the seminary. The group met every other week simply to tell our stories through the aid of four questions.

1. Describe a key experience in your life.

2. Describe a key relationship in your life.

3. What do you perceive to be a personal fear or weakness?

4. If you could wave your magic wand, what would you love to do with your life?

We never prodded anyone to share their story. We agreed to speak "as the Spirit moved." It would be one person's turn each week to work their way through the questions, while the rest of us listened for the common threads in the responses. On one memorable morning, Jaquie knew it was her turn. Unwittingly, she tied the first three questions into one story. A story of fear, pain and embarrassment began to flow from her as she told of the abuse she received from her father as a little girl. Repeatedly her father violated her young body and tragically bruised her spirit. She carried the scars in her mind long after they healed from her young body. Instead of understanding herself as the competent woman she was, Jaquie carried within herself a mental image of perceived weakness and incompetence.

Her perceived weakness became painfully evident to us that day as she painted a picture of her gripping fear that she would not be a competent mother for her own daughter and, even worse, that the same damaging abuse might happen to her own innocent child. Little did we know that the courage she exhibited in telling her story would set the pace for rest of the group. We sat in amazement as others in the group began to take courage and tell their own painful and anguished stories.

The transforming moment yet to come, however, was the startling surprise of the day. As ordinary people began to share the stories of their personal past, the mood of the group changed from despair to hope—a hope that recognized a connection between the pain of their stories and the passion of their callings. Ordinary stories became moments for extraordinary healing and koinonia. And even more, in the telling of their stories, people were helped to see their lives transformed by grace from broken, shameful, painful histories into competent, grace-energized, purpose-directed ministries to be shared with others.

Jaquie helped us recognize that we were attractive people. We were attractive because God had touched and graced our stories with uniqueness, forgiveness and purpose. It is no secret that today she brings a sense of competence, joy and purpose to her role of working with abused children. Jaquie now has a magnetic attraction for those who have journeyed through similar dark places. She is learning the joy that comes from having the courage to follow her call—a call that understands ministry as something that grows strong out of weakness.

One of the temptations facing people in vocational ministry today is the warped perception that they can handle the demands of ministry on their own. A well-respected pastor was asked, "To whom do you go with your questions, frustrations and victories?" His response is representative of a dangerously high proportion of clergy: "Why, I have no one to go to. I do ministry on my own."

Leadership studies among Christian leaders of various levels reveal that people who consider themselves to have finished well in ministry have had several mentoring relationships throughout their ministry. Conversely, one of the most common characteristics among those in ministry who did not finish well was a lack of mentoring relationships during their ministry tenure.[7] The value Augustine placed on having confessors is a healthy prescription for those who run in the race of faith with the intention of finishing the race well.

For Augustine, an attractive mentor was one who lived a holy life, was well experienced in an intimate relationship with God and had experience in life and ministry. The attractive life was also one where discernment, love and encouragement were provided in a creatively hospitable atmosphere of acceptance and trust. The character of the mentor, not the technical skill or academic background, was most important to Augustine.

One of the greatest spiritual writers of history, Teresa of Ávila, experienced what some call "the second conversion," a deepening of faith and spirituality, because she read the writings of Augustine. As she pored over his

his *Confessions*, she said her heart was broken at the vision of the wounded Christ. "As I began to read the *Confessions*, it seemed to me I saw myself in them."[8] She said she threw herself down in a torrent of tears. As will be described later, the circle of mentoring spiraled inexorably onward as Teresa's life both attracted and mentored a young monastic who chose the name John of the Cross. The imitative life of faith is duplicated in lives that will be reproduced in the lives of still others. Such is the wonder of spiritual mentoring.

For Reflection

☐ What do you need in order to claim your story?

☐ What keeps you from seeking out a spiritual mentor?

☐ What aspects of your life are attractable?

☐ Whom do you need to mentor spiritually?

☐ How would you establish expectations and boundaries?

Covenant Making

The spiritual disciplines practiced across the centuries all suggest a need for covenant making between mentor and spiritual seeker in order to establish the relationship. Covenant making is one of the ways God offered a relationship of intimacy to people under the old covenant and through Jesus in the new covenant of the Gospels. The biblical practice of covenant making offers a very practical tool for an early stage of the mentoring relationship. If attraction is the first step on the journey toward spiritual mentoring, we suggest that covenant making or establishment is the next discrete step in the process. A covenant is not a contract but rather a very practical agreement between two or more parties that is binding on all parties because both sides have agreed to the obligations specified in the agreement. The covenant will specify some of the practical "housekeeping" agreements between mentor and mentoree. Some prefer for this to remain unspoken, but we believe it is best when the covenant agreements are spoken aloud or even written. Some of the practical needs that must be outlined in a covenant for a spiritual mentoring relationship are outlined below.

1. Why?

☐ *Motivation* answers questions about why you are interested in a mentoring relationship.

2. Where? When?
   - ☐ *Location* answers questions of where to meet, in public or private.
   - ☐ *Frequency* answers questions of duration and intervals for meeting.
3. How?
   - ☐ *Format* answers questions of structure for utilization of time.
   - ☐ *Accountability* answers questions of disciplines and assignments.
   - ☐ *Confidentiality* answers questions of how privacy is maintained.
   - ☐ *Evaluation* answers questions of progress and expectations.
   - ☐ *Closure* answers questions of satisfactory completion of relationship.

Whether this covenant is written or verbal, it is valuable for both mentor and mentoree to understand each other's intentions and expectations for meeting. The intentionality of a covenant will bring some formality to what may remain an informal relationship. A covenant brings helpful structure to expectations so that anticipation is heightened appropriately. In our work on campuses, when we are approached by someone who desires a relationship of mentoring, we each ask a series of questions of ourselves and of the one who has sought us out. These include why, what, when, where and how questions. The following questions are written with the mentor in mind. They suggest valuable questions to be raised by the mentor in the early stage of work with a mentoree.

Why? Why me? What *motivates* you to choose me as a potential mentor? What do you know about me or assume about me that has led you to my doorstep? We use these questions to help the seeker evaluate perceptions and to assess the accuracy of those perceptions.

Why you? What *motivates* you to seek a more intentional process of mentoring with me or with anyone for that matter? A friend often asks an invaluable but brutally honest question, "What is the underlying self-interest for you in this request?" This question challenges the seeker to assess his or her motivation. Is this request compelled by guilt or a knee-jerk response to a recent sermon, conference or article? How ready is this person to commit to the work and the discipline that will be involved?

Why now? This is another way to press the issue of *motivation*. We want seekers to consider carefully and well their inner teachability. One of the most honest evaluations ever spoken to Keith came after a year of spiritual direction when he was told, "I don't believe you are ready for this in your life at this time." The words were not words of judgment and condemnation but rather words of honest appraisal of readiness.

What? What kind of relationship and process are you seeking? Some people are lonely and need a friend. Others want to be near someone they perceive to be a person of status, authority or competence. Some, like the woman in Mark's Gospel, simply want to draw some healing by "touching the hem" of a mentor's garment. So it must become clear what the seeker desires in a relationship. Often these are the most awkward moments in the conversation, because these seekers bring a sense of longing for something more or a desire for conversation and help, but they cannot articulate their needs. The purpose is not to find a "correct answer" from someone, but it is necessary to listen carefully as the seeker explains the desired relationship and process. "What would you envision us doing if we were to spend time together?"

Where, when and how? Once the preceding questions are answered, the questions of where, when, and how will become clear.

It is important to consider carefully a *location* for meeting, the question of where. Is an office the best place? Is there sufficient privacy and confidentiality? Is a restaurant acceptable for the depth of emotion and listening that needs to occur? Is the location comfortable but not distracting? Privacy and confidentiality are important considerations in the selection of location.

The question of *when* address the issues of *frequency* and *closure*. It is important to consider time and duration of meetings, in other words the *frequency* with which the mentoring meetings will take place. Will we meet weekly, more often or less? Will we schedule an hour once a week or a longer time less often? When also relates to question of *closure*. When will we evaluate and bring closure to this formal mentoring relationship? This will obviously be determined in part by the process chosen and activity planned, but it is important to talk about this question. How will we know when we have completed our work together?

The question of *how* addresses the actual process to be followed in terms of *format, accountability, confidentiality and evaluation.* Will a book be read by one or both during the times apart? How will prayer be used in the meeting times? Will a series of consistent questions for accountability be used as starters for the discussion? Will journaling be an expected part of the process? Will journal entries be shared? Will others be invited in for all or parts of the process (for example, spouse or special friends)? What level of confidentiality do we want to maintain? How will we evaluate the success of the mentoring relationship, and how often will we evaluate? Will we follow some of the Ignatian exercises described later? What about using the pattern of Jeanne

Guyon and her ideas about prayer? Will we use the method of *lectio divina*, also described in a later chapter? (All of these approaches are discussed in chapter six.)

Establishing Clear Boundaries

Aelred of Rievaulx, a twelfth-century exemplar of spiritual friendship, insisted on the importance of establishing boundaries when considering such an intimate relationship as spiritual friendship. One of Aelred's primary sources of attraction was none other than Augustine. Although Aelred placed a greater significance on the value of human relationship than Augustine discusses in *Confessions*, Aelred's classic work, *Spiritual Friendship*, reflects an Augustinian structure.[9]

Establishing clear boundaries can help the mentor assess in the attraction phase whether to enter into a covenant with someone desiring a relationship. Aelred's advice comes from an ongoing interaction with two monks named Walter and Gratian who sought him out for spiritual guidance.[10] Three helpful instructions reflect Aelred's wisdom for spiritual mentoring relationships today.

Avoid aimless relationships. Aelred gives a strong warning not to begin a spiritual mentoring relationship if it is based solely on affection without reason. Authentic discernment of the already present action of God will be hindered by both mentor and mentoree without a measure of reason and purpose to the relationship. "The beginnings of spiritual friendship ought to possess, first of all, purity of intention, the direction of reason and the restraint of moderation."[11] "I'd like to meet with you" may be a good first step, but Aelred would counsel us to think carefully about *purposeful* meetings.

Avoid evil relationships. Aelred warned his two mentorees not to enter relationships with an evil intent, which in his estimation are not worthy of the name friendship. Included in this category would be dishonorable acts that are detrimental to faith and uprightness for the sake of preserving the friendship. Am I motivated by anything that might become detrimental to this person's growth? Is there a morbid kind of curiosity about this person and the person's problems or history? Can this person give me information about someone else who might have hurt me in the past? Discernment of your intentions as mentor is essential.

Avoid self-seeking relationships. Mentors must always be careful about their own motivations in this work. Entering a relationship because there might be some strong personal benefit should be avoided. "For he has not yet learned what friendship is who wishes any reward other than itself. Such a reward friendship will certainly be for those cultivating it, when, wholly translated to God, it immerses in the divine contemplation those whom it has united."[12]

These are important guidelines for us in the early stage of covenant making. Friendships begin in numerous ways. They develop over time as people go deeper into intimacy and trust with each other. We have come to see that beginning well in a spiritual mentoring relationship requires paying attention to the life of another. You may be attracted to someone who might become your mentor. You may be drawn to a potential mentoree to accompany that person in the next step of a spiritual journey. We have also come to understand the benefit of bringing intentionality to a spiritual mentoring relationship by way of establishing a covenant. Now that the attraction dynamic has been established, it is time to explore how a hospitality of trust and intimacy can be cultivated in order for the spiritual mentoring relationship to mature.

Further Reflection for the Mentor

1. Attend to your own spiritual health and nourishment. Who is the mentor for you as mentor?

2. Who are those who might be ready to move more deeply into spiritual formation?

3. Is God nudging you to notice any particular person?

Further Reflection for the Mentoree

1. Pray. The place to begin the search for a spiritual mentor is the place the search will end—in the intentions of God's Spirit. Ask God to help you pay attention to someone you are attracted to for spiritual formation.

2. Practice the spirituality of discernment. In Matthew 13 Jesus remembers Isaiah's discernment that his people listened without understanding and looked without perceiving; their hearts had become dull. Their ears were deaf and they had shut their eyes. Pay attention.

3. Many people begin the spiritual discipline of keeping a journal of their spiritual biography, questions and prayers. You might wish to consider starting a simple journal in which you practice memory about the events and meaning of the day. The journal is a simple instrument that can facilitate paying attention.

Four

Developing
Trust & Intimacy
Relationship

Here we are, you and I, and I hope a third,
Christ, is in our midst. . . .
Come now, beloved, open your heart,
and pour into these friendly ears whatsoever you will,
and let us accept gracefully the boon of this place, time and leisure.

AELRED OF RIEVAULX

Nothing quite like a cup of coffee and an apple fritter. At least it certainly helps set the tone for intimate moments where memories are made. Every other Tuesday morning at ten they gathered together for spiritual mentoring. They were a group of eight who desired something more in their Christian walk. Randy tells the story:

Although I met with several of the men for individual times of spiritual mentoring, I wanted us to experience the coming together of our stories. I also wanted to mentor these men in the ways of spiritual mentoring so they would become empowered to do the same for others in their own communities. We met in my small, yet adequate, office. The walls are lined with books and there is a large window that catches the sometimes haunting, howling sounds of the South Dakota winds. There are two pictures on the wall: one shows me crossing the finish line at my first marathon in Duluth, Minnesota; the other is a picture of Edward Hopper's famous painting *Nighthawks*. This painting always invites me to jump into the picture and ask the lonesome characters in the coffee shop, "So, what's your story?" which, by the way, is perhaps the primary question we need to ask in spiritual mentoring.

In order for us to understand each other there needed to be an atmosphere conducive to the telling of our stories. It was my task as group leader to create a safe and hospitable space where their stories could fully be heard. Setting the tone meant being sensitive to places where trust and intimacy had somehow been violated with each of the guys. It also meant helping to remove the masks, if there were facades being worn, in order to get to the real persons. I knew that I needed to proceed in a priestly way with appropriate questions and exercises.

We met because we wanted to make sense of our lives and gain some divine direction for the next phase of our journeys. Three questions often surfaced in our times together: Where was God when . . . ? Who am I? What does God desire to do through me now?

Telling our stories was not simply an exercise in memory sharing: recalling life-changing moments, both good and bad, or swapping battlefield experiences. It was rather a time for each of us to recognize the already present action of God in the stories of our lives. As we told those stories, friendships already begun moved deeper, trust already present became greater, and intimacy already known became profoundly more vulnerable. What started in the early stages of attraction and covenant making was moving now into a later phase of developing increased trust and intimacy.

In this chapter we will talk about developing trust and intimacy between mentor and mentoree, a dynamic that is simply called *relationship*. Robert Clinton defines the relationship dynamic as "a growing interactive trust between mentor and mentoree which is the basis upon which responsiveness, and accountability will function and which will eventuate in empowerment."[1]

Once the process has begun in the initial phase of attraction, what is necessary to sustain the spiritual mentoring relationship in the life of the mentoree? We will suggest two working metaphors to describe the process of developing trust and intimacy—friendship and hospitality. This process does not involve magic or rocket science; it does require the practice of two everyday relational skills. The development of trust and intimacy is the foundation of the relationship and the responsibility of both the mentor and the mentored. It involves a lively interaction of trust offered and trust accepted by two people who are moving toward an intimate and deep relationship. Trust is developed through listening, for listening is to love what breathing is to life itself. Trust is earned through care given to the trust offered. Trust emerges through the development of friendship and hospitality.

The dynamic of relationship is foundational in the art of spiritual mentoring. Sensitive fostering of trust and intimacy in timely fashion is a crucial link in a spiritual mentoring process that allows accountability and responsiveness to give way to empowerment. But how do you trust someone with your deepest identity when your life history caused a paralysis that prevents trust? It is only in the safety of a trusting, intimate relationship that you will be able to learn to trust again. We speak of this as "creating a safe space." But what does such a "safe space" look like?

Creating a Safe Space for Discovery

What we're talking about in the early stages of the relationship of spiritual mentoring has elsewhere been described as "developing a hospitable learning environment."[2] It is a place where learning is welcomed, growth is honored and trustful intimacy is desired. In his book *To Know As We Are Known* Parker Palmer refers to a learning space as a place of heart and mind as well of physical location. His phrase "spirituality of education" is very close to what we mean by the spirituality of the mentoring relationship.

Palmer has come to believe that three characteristics are necessary for the development of learning spaces: openness, boundaries and hospitality. "Openness" refers to the removal of impediments to learning. These impediments may be in the physical space in which teaching and learning occur, but they may just as likely be impediments of mistrust, negativity, stereotyping and fear. By "boundaries" Palmer means that a learning space needs to have limits. For the teacher and learner to feel safe, certain boundaries are created. Boundaries of time and schedule, trust and confidentiality are examples. "Hospitality" refers to receiving each other as guests and welcoming each other as honored visitors. It means that we each receive the other with openness and care as each one arrives with struggles and questions. We do what it takes to create an environment in which a community can be formed.[3]

Palmer recognizes that learning is more than simple rationality or emotionality. There is a spirituality to all learning, in which we come to know as we seek to be known. Seeking truth has to do with entering into a relationship, a covenant, with others in which we might learn together in an environment of trust and intimacy. A self-conscious and intentional responsibility of the mentor is the creation of an atmosphere in which the mentor knows that it is safe to explore, doubt and wonder. These are the tasks of the mentor in nurturing increased relationships of trust and intimacy:

☐ to create a space welcoming the mentoree to be safe and open

☐ to create a space with boundaries of confidentiality, structure and guidance

☐ to create a space where questions, struggles, emotions and doubts are welcome

☐ to create a space that fosters ideas, curiosity, wonder and joy

☐ to create a space that honors the mundane as containers of holy grace

The creation of a safe space is a continuing task in the process of spiritual mentoring. In this environment language is valued as two or more persons take seriously the spoken word that reveals the text of human life as it is lived in the messiness of Monday through Friday, as well as Saturday and Sunday. The safe place, rather than formulas, steps or procedures, will allow for discovery of trust and intimacy.

Any mentoree making progress on a spiritual pilgrimage with the help of a mentor will describe a mentoring setting where it is safe to talk. Most of us have learned to speak boldly with other people about things other than personal spirituality. We are free to talk about the passions we have for Starbucks coffee, the Chicago Cubs or Puget Sound, but we find ourselves more reserved in talking about relationships with God. We want to tell our life stories, but we wonder if the stories are too common, too confused, too carnal or just plain too complicated. It is the ongoing role of the mentor to create and nurture a safe place in which the mentoree can disclose his or her interior self to the mentor. For a relationship to grow into one of intimate trust, both mentor and mentoree must become vulnerable with sin, pain and questions related to living a life of holiness and service. The mentoree must learn to be responsive to the wisdom provided by the mentor if effective life changes are going to emerge. This means that the mentor is increasingly given permission to ask tough questions that will penetrate the masks most of us wear.

Assurances that "it's okay to talk" will fall like hollow echoes if the mentor is not a person who can hold confidences securely. Guarantees that "I won't tell another living soul" can sound like empty words if the mentor seems to exhibit too much curiosity about the story of the mentoree.

How trust develops is more like an art form than a recipe book. Trust and intimacy unfold in faltering steps or in the stuttering telling of stories as two people dare to reveal their most intimate spiritual selves to one another as friends.

In this chapter we're going to return to the twelfth century, to a monk named Aelred who wrote a book called *Spiritual Friendship*. His concept of the mentor as a spiritual friend offers significant and practical guidance for us in nurturing the mentoring relationship.

The Mentor as Friend

In the classical world of spiritual direction, the mentor was a guide, a director, a ruler and, sometimes, a figure of authority. Often mentors were monastics, priests or clergy scholars who were highly respected in their society. Today it is common for mentors to be acquaintances in informal relationships: teacher and students, coach and team, small groups of friends who meet for coffee and spiritual talk. They gather for prayer, fellowship and spiritual formation. Friendship and hospitality thus offer natural and comfortable settings for spiritual mentoring. Two spiritual teachers, Aelred of Rivaulx and Henri Nouwen, offer two practical metaphors that help us value the "daily sacrament" of spiritual friendship and teach us that friendship is the environment in which our souls are nurtured for spiritual formation.

In the twelfth century a young monk named Aelred reflected on the great Stoic philosopher Cicero's classic work *De Amicitia,* "On Friendship," and proposed his own ideas in a writing that he called *Spiritual Friendship.* To tell the story of Aelred, however, we must first speak of his friend Bernard of Clairvaux, for Bernard's role as friend/mentor shaped Aelred, his thought and his work.

At the young age of twenty-two, Bernard made his own decision to enter monastic life in his native land of England and started what would become his practice throughout all of his life—rather than enter the monastery alone he brought with him five family members, including four brothers and an uncle, and twenty-five other friends. This was to become a repeated pattern for this charismatic man who created the Cistercian movement. Bernard, who became the mentor of Aelred, William of St.-Thierry and dozens of others, created a movement whose intellectual and devotional truth needs to be rediscovered today. Simply stated, Bernard's belief was "Knowledge of God comes only through devotion to God, in poverty, in simplicity, and in solitude."[4]

In one of his *Sermons on the Song of Songs* Bernard wrote,

> The instructions that I address to you, my brothers, will differ from those I would address to those out in the world; at least, the manner would be different. . . . It is Paul's method of teaching . . . a more nourishing diet to those who are enlightened spiritually. . . . "We teach," he says, "not in the way philosophy is taught, but in the way the Holy Spirit teaches us; we teach spiritual things spiritually" (1 Cor. 2:13).[5]

Bernard was impressed by the writing abilities of young Aelred from the north England town of Hexham and pressed him to write his book *Spiritual Friendship*. Aelred's historic impact on the understanding of spiritual relationships was unprecedented. It is interesting to observe that his writings became more insightful after he ceased trying to write out of a philosophical framework and trusted his own experience and perspectives.

Aelred's life was punctuated by experiences of spiritual guidance that influenced his insight into friendship as a form of spiritual direction. His introduction to adulthood came through a common custom in the ancient feudal age. Sons of wealthy families would often receive a year of tutelage and training in the homes of other members of the upper class. This custom, called "fosterage," would train the young in matters appropriate to their status and create networks of friendship essential to their positions of power and responsibility. Aelred went, as a boy of fifteen, to the court of the king of Scots for his time of fosterage. His passage into young adulthood began with an experience of mentoring. Not surprisingly, his life ended similarly, with a circle of monks gathered around him as they often did for conversation, mentorship and friendship. He wrote of the contributions of friendship to one's depth of life. Three of his ideas about friendship give a taste of the depth of his thinking.

> For friendship bears fruit in this life and in the next.[6]
>
> But what happiness, what security, what joy to have someone to whom you dare to speak on terms of equality as to another self; one to

whom you need have no fear to confess your failings; one to whom you can unblushingly make known what progress you have made in the spiritual life; one to whom you can entrust all the secrets of your heart and before whom who can place all your plans! What, therefore, is more pleasant than so to unite to oneself the spirit of another and of two to form one, that no boasting is thereafter to be feared, no suspicion to be dreaded, no correction of one by the other to cause pain, no praise on the part of one to bring a charge of adulation from the other. "A friend," says the Wise Man, "is the medicine of life."[7]

Friendship, therefore, heightens the joys of prosperity and mitigates the sorrows of adversity by dividing and sharing them. Hence, the best medicine in life is a friend. Even the philosophers took pleasure in the thought: not even water, nor the sun, nor fire do we use in more instances than a friend. In every action in every pursuit, in certainty, in doubt, in every event and fortune of whatever sort, in private and in public, in every deliberation, at home and abroad, everywhere friendship is found to be appreciated, a friend a necessity, a friend's service a thing of utility. "Wherefore, friends," says Tullius, "though absent are present, though poor are rich, though weak are strong, and—what seems stranger still—though dead are alive." And so it is that the rich prize friendship as their glory, the exiles as their native land, the poor as their wealth, the sick as their medicine, the dead as their life, the healthy as their charm, the weak as their strength and the strong as their prize.[8]

Can one be taught intimate spiritual things outside the context of relationship? Bernard of Clairvaux would say no. Can one mentor another spiritually without the underlying basis of an intimate trusted friendship? Aelred would say no. Spiritual mentoring that imitates Jesus' style with his own disciples would say no. Spiritual mentoring is, in its very essence, a relationship of trust and emerging intimacy, a friendship shared with one another and with the Lord Jesus Christ. It may not be the friendship of shared social activities and events, but it is the friendship of the highest order, the friendship of shared hearts.

For Reflection
Take some moments to reflect on the value of your own friendships to your

spiritual development.
☐ How have your friendships formed, *mis*formed, *mal*formed or *trans*formed you as a person of faith?
☐ What practical benefits have your friendships provided your spiritual growth?
☐ Who have become your most trusted friends? Why? How did these friendships develop?

Stages of Friendship

Aelred taught that there are stages of friendship, which we believe are highly suggestive of "movements" in the mentoring relationship. There may not be strictly defined steps through which all relationships move, but Aelred emphatically stressed four fluid movements in the development of spiritual friendship: selection, probation, admission and harmony.

> A friend ought to be chosen with the utmost care and tested with extreme caution. But once admitted, he should be so borne with, so treated, so deferred to, that, as long as he does not withdraw irrevocably from the established foundation, he is yours and you are his, in body as well as in spirit, so that there will be no division of minds, affections, wills, or judgments. You see, therefore, the four stages by which one climbs to the perfection of friendship: the first is selection, the second probation, the third admission, and the fourth perfect harmony in matters human and divine with charity and benevolence.[9]

These movements in friendship help ensure the cultivation of trust and intimacy between two friends. For Aelred, love was the binding force to the relationship. "There can be love without friendship, but friendship without love is impossible."[10] Mentoring, like friendship, is a process. It takes work to develop trust and intimacy, and Aelred believed that friends moved through these four steps in order to acquire the trust and intimacy of the spiritually mature. Admittedly we seldom speak today of developing friendship so methodically, but Aelred understood that friendship is far too significant in our lives to be casual and capricious about it.

As you read his four steps, think about how this might be instructive for developing a mentoring relationship. Suggested questions follow each of his four steps in the development of spiritual friendship.

Selection. Aelred bids us look for several elements of love, affection, security and happiness in a spiritual friendship.

> Love implies the rendering of services with benevolence, affection and inward pleasure that manifests itself exteriorly; security, a revelation of all counsels and confidences without fear and suspicion; happiness, a pleasing and friendly sharing of all events which occur, whether joyful or sad, of all thoughts, whether harmful or useful, of everything taught or learned.[11]

☐ To whom are you attracted as mentor or mentoree? Which of Aelred's elements of friendship draw you to this person?

Probation. Aelred describes four personal characteristics that are tested in the early development of friendship.

> There are four qualities that must be *tested* in a friend: loyalty, right intention, discretion, and patience, that you may entrust yourself to him securely. The right intention, that he may expect nothing from your friendship except God and its natural good. Discretion, that he may understand what is to be done in behalf of a friend, what is be sought from a friend, what sufferings are to be endured for his sake, upon what good deeds he is to be congratulated; and, since we think that a friend should sometimes be corrected, he must know for what faults this should be done, as well as the manner, the time, and the place. Finally, patience, that he may not grieve when rebuked, or despise the one inflicting the rebuke, and that he may not be unwilling to bear adversity for the sake of his friend.[12]

☐ What steps might you take to create a spirit of trial and discernment for you as mentor and mentoree? How might you test the readiness of the mentoree for the serious work of spiritual mentoring?

Admission. Acquaintances who have been found trustworthy are then fully admitted to friendship.

> We embrace very many with every affection, but yet in such a way that we do not admit them to the secrets of friendship, which consists especially in the revelation of all our confidences and plans. . . . As Saint Ambrose says, "He gives the formula of friendship for

us to follow: namely, that we do the will of our friend, that we disclose
to our friend whatever confidences we have in our hearts, and that we
be not ignorant of his confidences. Let us lay bare to him our heart and
let him disclose his to us. For a friend hides nothing. If he is true, he
pours forth his soul just as the Lord Jesus poured forth the mysteries
of the Father." Thus speaks Ambrose. How many, therefore, do we love
before whom it would be imprudent to lay bare our souls and pour out
our inner hearts! men whose age or feeling or discretion is not sufficient
to bear such revelations.[13]

☐ Is there evidence of growing trust and vulnerability in your times of
mentoring? In what ways can you see a deepening friendship growing
between you?

Harmony. Continuing friendship can then develop into a more profound
relationship.

> Let a man, therefore, conform and adapt himself to his friend to be in
> harmony with his disposition. As one ought to be of aid to a friend in
> his material setbacks, so he ought the more readily hasten to succor him
> in trials of the spirit.[14]
>
> How advantageous it is then to grieve for one another, to toil for one
> another to bear one another's burdens, while each considers it sweet to
> forget himself for the sake of the other, to prefer the will of the other to
> his own, to minister to the other's needs rather than one's own, to oppose
> and expose oneself to misfortunes! Meanwhile, how delightful friends
> find it to converse with one another, mutually to reveal their interests,
> to examine all things together, and to agree on all of them! Added to
> this there is prayer for one another, which coming from a friend, is the
> more efficacious in proportion as it is more lovingly sent to God, with
> tears which either fear excites or affection awakens or sorrow evokes.[15]

☐ Do you both eagerly anticipate your scheduled times? How have your
prayers for one another deepened as your work together has deepened?

Aelred thought of friendship as the very heart of spiritual guidance. In
fact, he doesn't seem to think that spiritual guidance will happen apart from
the love of friend for friend. Today the word *friendship* is used much more
casually. Friends may be those with whom we work or ride an elevator to our

office; they may be acquaintances or neighbors whom we see only across the alley or at the grocery store. For Aelred, a friend was someone to be loved and cared for, one with whom he desired to grow in faith and ministry.

For Reflection

☐ What becomes different in the development of trust and intimacy with your mentoree if you think of this person as a friend and of your spiritual responsibility as friendship?

☐ How do you nurture trust in your most important relationships?

☐ What has worked for you in the development of intimacy with your closest and deepest friends?

☐ How might those practices transfer from friendship to your role as a spiritual mentor?

Several irreducible basics appear in almost all deep friendships:

☐ the practice of careful, engaged listening

☐ the practice of thoughtful, interested question-asking

☐ the practice of confidentiality in which the privacy of friends is honored

☐ the practice of progressive trust-giving and trust-receiving between friends

The Mentor as Host

The prophetic scholar-priest Henri Nouwen often connected hospitality and ministry as metaphors of great importance. He understood hospitality as the process of creating a free and open space in which people can meet without fear or hostility. So offering hospitality has great significance for spiritual development.

> Although many, we might even say most, strangers in this world become easily the victim of a fearful hostility, it is possible for men and women and obligatory for Christians to offer an open and hospitable space where strangers can cast off their strangeness and become our fellow human beings.... That is our vocation: to convert the *hostis* into a *hospes*, the enemy into a guest and to create the free and fearless space where brotherhood and sisterhood can be formed and fully experienced.[16]

Hospitality then is a ministry of friends who open lives, homes and hearts to others for their refreshment, nurture, growth and enjoyment. Just as Aelred spoke of spiritual friendship as a virtue to be treasured, so Nouwen spoke of hospitality as a biblical vocation for which the Christian is uniquely suited.

> When hostility is converted into hospitality then fearful strangers can become guests revealing to their hosts the promise they are carrying with them. Then, in fact, the distinction between host and guest proves to be artificial and evaporates in the recognition of the newfound unity. Thus the biblical stories help us to realize not just that hospitality is an important virtue but even more that in the context of hospitality guest and host can reveal their most precious gifts and bring new life to each other.[17]

Elsewhere Nouwen adds,

> Perhaps teachers cannot be true teachers unless they are to a certain degree friends. In other words, when Jesus said to his disciples, "I shall no longer call you servants; . . . I call you friends" (Jn 15:15), he became in truth their real teacher because all fear was overcome and real learning could begin.[18]

Those who personally knew Nouwen say that he was a man who longed for a sense of home, a place of hospitality where he could be fully heard, fully accepted, fully loved for the man he was. It seems he found such a hospitable space in his dearly loved friend Adam. Adam was a severely handicapped young man who lived at the L'Arche Daybreak Community.

Nouwen's transition from the prestigious Harvard to the live-in community of L'Arche was anything but easy. His first responsibility in his new residence was providing very intimate care for Adam, one of his housemates. Through this paradoxical relationship Nouwen came to discover the truth of his own belovedness. His words present to us a holy calling to recognize our belovedness through the presence of a spiritual mentor—through one like Adam.

> In our society plagued by fear, anxiety, loneliness, depression, and a sense of being lost, we keep looking for guides. We so much hope that someone—a guru, spiritual director, or soul friend—can help us make sense out of our confusion and can show us a way to inner wholeness, freedom, and peace. We look mostly for men and women with a

reputation, with wisdom, psychological insight, spiritual sensitivity, and solid life experience. Perhaps the problem is that we expect too much, and they want to give too much. Then we become dependent and they become controlling. Adam was the least controlling and the most dependent guide I ever encountered. Maybe that's why I was able to put so much confidence in his way. I believe he worked miracles like the miracles of Jesus precisely because he never claimed any of them for himself. He didn't ask for money, fame, or even thanks. In his total powerlessness Adam was a pure instrument of God's healing power ... for me.[19]

In the mutual sharing of friendship and hospitality, spiritual formation occurs in natural and holistic ways. Both Aelred and Nouwen help us see mentoring as a process of spiritual friendship, creating hospitality for God, the mentoree and the mentor. While some are uniquely gifted in the skills of friendship and hospitality, the church nurtures spiritual friendship in an atmosphere where friendship and hospitality flow naturally in relationships, regardless of our capacity. Adam's gift to Nouwen was a hospitality of unconditional friendship—a space freely provided where love was both given and received. We are captivated by the accessibility and suggestiveness of these metaphors for the second movement in spiritual mentoring. We all have friends and have experienced hospitality as either host or guest. The movements of spiritual mentoring follow closely the movements of friendship and hospitality—we open home or self to others in progressive steps of honesty, trust, intimacy and vulnerability.

The Courage of Vulnerability

The safe, hospitable space of trust and intimacy will never become a reality unless the mentor, leader, preacher or teacher becomes vulnerable. In our study of the historical writers we began to notice that mentoring relationships were not based on training, education or esoteric knowledge but were found in character, heart, experience, wisdom and discernment. Learning was sharing—of stories, questions, insights, confusion, suffering, paradox and joy Discernment was not given; it was shared. Wisdom was not imposed; it was portrayed. Character was not taught; it was evoked. As mentors we exercise the courage of vulnerability to offer our lives and experiences, our integrity and failures, our understanding and confusion so that both partners in the relationship can learn. In the courage of vulnerability, the mentor dares to set aside power and defensiveness. When a mentor becomes vulnerable he or she takes off the mask and dares to open up his or her own story—in its unedited version—but only when doing so will free the mentoree to share as well. Vulnerability is not a license to describe every experience of the mentoree through the previous experience of the mentor. "Let me tell you all about how it was for me" is a dangerous direction for a mentor to go. There must be wise discernment about the appropriate time to interject the mentor's own stories into the conversation.

What the mentor shares most personally is not a technique of instruction but a space for relationship to happen so that attentive learning might be possible. What Jesus showed us in the most dramatic of all incarnations was a self-emptying, a *kenosis* of power and status so that he could become incarnationally available to people. When Paul used the *kenosis* word of Jesus' ministry, he said that Jesus "emptied himself" in order to become one with us. Incarnational availability is *kenosis* work, which requires truth telling between mentor and mentoree. Aelred spoke with brevity, "Indeed, a man owes truth to his friend, without which the name of friendship has no value."[20]

When he wrote his book on ministry, Henri Nouwen called it *The Wounded Healer* because he understood that only those whose own hearts have been wounded by the suffering of life can be authentically available to others; it is through telling our own histories of pain and joy that we can serve the needs of others, which is ministry. A mentor will increasingly learn to share personal stories in the way that a good host shares his experiences of the city that is visited by his guest, not obtrusively or demanding that the guest duplicate the experience of the host, but freely and willingly. The mentor believes that new life can be found through the life lived and shared with the mentoree. The mentor must have the courage to become vulnerable with the mentoree in the journey of the relationship. And the mentor will have an ability to look beyond the present, not because of an optimistic personality but because of an understanding that God is the Lord of resurrection and Easter hope.

Keith remembers a particularly trying time in his seminary years:

I sat in the office of my mentor, my friend. Many times before he had guided me to answers, solutions, explanations and wisdom. His words usually flowed easily and rapidly, filled with suggestions for my skill development, but this day he was quiet, his hands folded together on his desk. He then stood and walked around the room. He said, "The great preacher Harry Emerson Fosdick had a strong influence on my life, you know. His sermons are some of the best from his era in American history. What you don't likely know is that he suffered a nervous breakdown at a crucial point in his development as a young man, an experience that molded his preaching for the rest of this life." The history lesson was intriguing, but I didn't have to wait long for the point. "In my college years, I too experienced something like that." During the next hour he slowly revealed his own story of trauma, confusion, pain and distress, taking care to answer my surprised and stumbling questions.

There were no answers given that day—or were there? No solution was offered to my problems. No guidelines for final resolution, no wisdom that would show me the way. That day a skilled and competent man was a courageous mentor. He discerned the difference between teaching me skills and showing me life. He discerned when it was time to tell me what I needed to hear and when it was time to be vulnerable and say, "No answers today—just a story." In the stories he told, especially of detours on his own pilgrimage, he created hospitality for me as he invited me to join him and a great preacher of history at the table of not knowing. While listening and asking pertinent questions is valuable, times for courageous and vulnerable personal sharing are needed for the good of the mentoree and of the relationship.

For Reflection
☐ How vulnerable are you with those whom you seek to mentor?
☐ What would it look like for you to be "emptied of yourself"?
☐ Where in your life do you desire to be powerful?

Four Major Pitfalls for the Spiritual Mentor to Avoid
☐ The Messiah Complex: I believe I am to rescue you or deliver you from the struggles and pain of your life.
☐ The Problem-Solver Mentality: I believe my role is to tell you what the right answers are or to offer a way out for you.

☐ The Assembly-Line Syndrome: I believe my role is to shape you into a predetermined form or product.

☐ The Wisdom Dispenser Approach: I believe I must dispense wisdom-on-demand every time I meet with my mentoree, because I am a fountain of wisdom and truth.

When a mentor becomes messiah, problem-solver, assembly-line worker or wisdom-dispenser, the opportunity for spiritual formation can become limited. A mentor is none of these four, though problem solving, wisdom and answers may be part of the unfolding process. Discernment is the pearl of great price for the mentor. Attaining discernment requires vulnerability, humility and an ear open to listen to the voice of God's spirit.

Essential Functions for Developing Friendship and Hospitality

How is the relationship developed through the early times of meeting and sharing conversation? Spiritual mentoring as friendship and hospitality will concentrate on three essential functions of the mentor:

☐ Holy Listening: giving attention, developing companionship, enjoying friendship, traveling the road together with the mentoree aware of the Holy Spirit in all places.

☐ Holy Seeing: observing the other with love, compassion, genuine care, concern and interest in the development of the mentoree.

☐ Wholly Listening: being fully and authentically present to the spiritual seeker and the Holy Spirit, daring the courage of a vulnerability that appropriately self-discloses to the mentoree, a vulnerability in which all of me listens to all of you.

Holy listening. Just as Jesus taught through the informality of life "on the way," so mentoring helps us listen to life "on the way." There is a dreadful and damaging notion in the church that spiritual things happen only when we're at church or in worship or when the clergy is involved. We believe God will communicate in all of these times, but the music of the soul is learned just as a child learns to sing, "on the way." Does the child wait until the singing lessons or the recital to raise his voice in song? Does she hold her tongue until it is deemed the "right time" for music? There are no limits placed by the Holy Spirit on times, places and moments when our souls can learn to sing. The helpful imagery of parental conversation from Deuteronomy 6 offers a powerful description of the earthiness and practicality of learning spirituality "on the way."

Keep these words that I am commanding you today in your heart. Recite them to your children and talk about them when you are at home and when you are away, when you lie down and when you rise. Bind them as a sign on your hand, fix them as an emblem on your forehead, and write them on the doorposts of your house and on your gates. (Deut 6:6-9)

Hebrew parents had a passion that their children would know certain truths about their God, Yahweh. They were insistent that children learn to remember and recite the music of their history and its incarnated theology. They understood, as well, that learning was somehow to be connected to the experience of their children's lives. Thus numerous postures of learning are described: sitting, lying down, walking, standing. Children were encouraged to pay attention to their lives in all its earthiness. The curriculum was an ever-unfolding syllabus of questions, doubts and frustrations. Without using the language of learning, they educated their children in the midst of life experience. Children learn what they live. Children will learn to sing the songs of faith if they are taught in the natural and responsive moments "on the way."

Hebrew parents further understood that spiritual education needed to take place in a relationship of familiarity and love. Learning about faith was never intended to be an academic pursuit, disconnected from family and life, taught conceptually and in abstraction. Rather, learning about faith is a natural, unfolding, pragmatic, holistic process of discovery in the concrete moments of life itself. It occurred most naturally in the safety and creative learning space of the Hebrew home.

Finally, they understood that teaching required a passion for something of great importance and conviction in their lives. No Hebrew parent would approach the task with indifference; to tell the story to the next generation was a vital, essential stewardship. In the Hebrew language, *know* was a word richly nuanced with intimacy. To know meant to be committed. To know meant to care. To know meant vulnerability. It implied an intimacy born of passionate commitment to the ones being taught.

This is not to suggest that mentoring should take on a parental tone or relationship; in fact, the authoritarian approach of some parental mentoring may lead to a mentoree's dependency rather than the empowerment of the mentoree's own voice. It is to suggest, however, that mentoring is deeply relational, wisely alert to the movement of God in the dailyness of life and anchored in a passionate love for God and the growth of the mentoree. It means that we will reconnect that which has become disconnected, re-member that which has become *dis*membered through separation of faith from life, learning from life, teaching from life. That is why the development of a relationship of trust is essential for mentoring. As the Hebrew family discovered truth in the context of trust, intimacy and vulnerability, so too will truth be discovered in a spiritual mentoring relationship where a hospitable space of intimacy and vulnerability has been created.

Paying attention, for mentor and mentoree, is learning to listen to the voice of God, which can become more real than the audible tones of other sounds that surround us and assault us all day, every day. Paying attention draws us into the sound of God's still small voice within the life of the soul. When our imaginations become thoroughly God-attentive, we will have freed our souls to sing. In spiritual mentoring we are helped to cultivate an ear that listens, an eye that sees, a soul that sings: this is a God-attentive life.

Now here's the surprising thing: the holy is commonly experienced in that which is not God.

Holy mountains, sacred song and holy *places*—sanctuaries. In all cultures and times we have the witness of story, song and ritual honoring this mysterious and divine otherness in things and people who are very much present, here and now. . . . Poets and artists regularly call our attention to the holy in various and sometimes surprising places.[21]

Holy listening is learning to hear the still, small voice of God—in daily, unexpected and common places. In a course in the city of Chicago students are read a poem from the writer and sociologist Andrew Greeley, who says, "In Chicago our God lurks everywhere."[22] Some people don't like the idea of God lurking behind dumpsters and in alleys, or sneaking up on them in a coffee shop or on the job, but the image works well for our understanding of spirituality. God is out there waiting to ambush us with love and the gift of the divine presence, and God invites us to pay attention.

Do you know what the great fictional detective Sherlock Holmes said was the reason most people were not good detectives? "You see, but you do not observe." If we want to notice the surrounding signs of the presence of God, we need to slow down our lives enough to observe. Then we will learn to see the activity of the Unseen God in the midst of that which we see. We need someone to help us see—a mentor who can help us see spiritually.

Holy seeing. The Old Testament story of 2 Kings 6 stirs us to ask, what does it mean to experience God, to know God, to be known by God? To understand this text, it might be helpful to take you back to Keith's childhood in Chicago.

> You have to picture an eight-year-old freckle-faced redheaded kid with huge ears and a cool flattop haircut. Thick, heavy, brown corduroy pants (kind of like Abercrombie now sells for about two thousand dollars a pair) and a wild, very in, shirt with polka dots or little cars or trains or something very classy. There I am on Saturday morning looking at the television. Cartoons are okay, but I wait for the Roy Rogers show because my dad met one of the actors downtown at lunch one day—the old guy with the hugest beard in the world—Gabby Hayes. He was always getting in trouble, getting caught by the bad guys and getting tied up to a chair in the Silver Dollar Saloon. Roy Rogers would have to rush in on his horse Trigger to rescue Gabby or Gabby and Dale Evans or Gabby and some other helpless female character. I would be glued to the set, though I knew the outcome well in advance.

In 2 Kings 6 the characters are different, but the plot is the same. The prophet Elisha was in trouble. The king of Aram or Syria would mount a secret plot to bring down his enemy, the king of Israel, but Elisha would know about the plot because God spoke to him and he would tell the king who could then cleverly avoid the ambush. Finally the Syrian king gathered all his people together and demanded to know who was telling their secret plans. So the king set up another ambush and surrounded the prophet's house in Dothan, where Elisha lived with his young servant.

Verse 15 could be a line from Gabby Hayes himself, in his best dramatic voice. Before the servant had time to get the Starbucks coffee made in the morning he looked out the window and saw that they were surrounded by soldiers and that those soldiers were not waving the flag for the home team! So he ran to his master in fear and trembling, "Alas, master! What shall we do?"

Elisha was calm and said to him, "Don't sweat it. There are more of them on our side than on theirs." At this point the young servant boy had more to worry about than before. His house was surrounded by enemy troops, and now his master had lost his ability to do basic functional math! They were 1 + 1 against a whole army, and Elisha said, "Do not be afraid, for there are more with us than there are with them."

Verse 17 describes the pivotal event in the entire episode as Elisha prays a prayer to God for vision. "O Lord, please open his eyes that he may see." And when the servant boy looked again he saw what the prophet saw with the eyes of faith; he saw the mountains full of horses and chariots of fire surrounding the house of Elisha.

The biblical teaching is clear and repeated often: Faith is a way of seeing. It is a way of opening our eyes to see the world as God sees it. That is the spiritual journey we are taking—a journey to ask God to open our eyes so we may see what is there—spiritual forces of power that are mighty and invincible, but invisible to the human eye. We read in Hebrews 11:1 that "faith is the assurance of things hoped for, the conviction of things not seen." Faith isn't blind—it is the opposite. Faith is a spiritual way of seeing what our physical eyes alone will never see on their own. "By faith we understand that the worlds were prepared by the word of God, so that what is seen was made from things that are not visible" (Heb 11:3).

Good scientific reasoning doesn't like that sequence very much. We normally draw conclusions about what we don't see physically based on what we do see. We gather the evidence of what we know and then infer what we don't know. The gospel's way of knowing reverses that as God awakens our spiritual senses so that we are enabled to understand what we see based on what we don't see.

When and where do we see God? In the Bible, God is often revealed in the ordinary routine of daily life. Many of us think we must perceive God as the result of some mystical, almost hallucinatory experience, or in some holy place—a monastery, a sanctuary, on a mountaintop, or during some quiet retreat. But God met Moses while he was doing what he did every day—keeping sheep. As we said, Isaiah had his great vision of God while worshiping. Paul was traveling and Mary was drawing water. The disciples were mending their nets and taking care of their everyday fishing chores when Jesus called them, saying, "Follow me."

Wholly listening. Margaret Guenther has written that spiritual direction is sustained and nurtured best through all stages of the relationship by uncovering the obvious in our lives. Spiritual mentoring is, therefore, about *wholly* listening. When the mentor is able to listen *wholly, holy* listening occurs. Perhaps the most important quality of the mentor is the person's ability to help others listen to their own lives. Spiritual mentoring is not intended to be a substitute for psychotherapy or counseling but rather an occasion for holy listening by wholly listening.

Aelred understood spiritual direction as a time of holy listening to the already active presence of God when he wrote, "Here we are, you and I, and I hope a third, Christ, is in our midst."[23] Spiritual mentoring is the occasion for wholly listening to the third in our midst, an attentiveness that makes it holy listening. As companions on the journey, mentors intentionally and carefully help others listen to their own lives, ask their own questions, connect their own stories to The Story, Jesus' story. The mentoree is not idle or passive during the development of the mentoring relationship. The mentoree must learn to become skilled at the sacred work of holy listening to Christ "in our midst" by listening to the voice of the mentor, the voice of the Holy Spirit and the voice within.

God speaks to us in many ways. A commonly held view today equates our spirituality with our devotional life. If I have a great devotional life, then I have a great spiritual life. If my morning devotions were stellar than I must be close to God; if not, then my spiritual life is weak. If I "feel" God in my prayer life or if I "hear" God in almost auditory experience, if I "see" God in a mystical or charismatic vision, then my spiritual life is good, strong or effective. The universal teaching of spirituality over all the centuries speaks in unison: God speaks to us in many ways; *spirituality is learning to pay attention to the presence of God in everything.*

Spiritual listening is never limited to the activities of worship, daily devotions or spiritual exercises. It echoes in unexpected ways every hour of the day and night. How deeply, how wholly, we need to hear the words of David who wrote,

> The heavens are telling the glory of God;
> and the firmament proclaims his handiwork.
> Day to day pours forth speech,
> and night to night declares knowledge.
> There is no speech, nor are there words;
> their voice is not heard;
> yet their voice goes out through all the earth,
> and their words to the end of the world. (Ps 19:1-4)

David believed that creation in all its earthiness and ordinariness actually was a microphone for broadcasting the glory of God! Without words and without speech, "their voice goes out through all the earth." God's voice is proclaimed through the heavens as well as through the perfect decrees of God's law. David had faith to believe that through all of creation God breathed his loving words to humankind. We could say that God sang his song to the human family!

Teresa of Ávila taught that God is found among the pots and pans. She helped her community know that dramatic spiritual experiences are not intrinsically more valuable than the habitual obedience of day-by-day faithfulness. Spiritual maturity, or "perfection" as she called it, must be measured not by mystical moments but rather by doing God's will in the context of real life. She would like the text of 1 John 1:1-2:

> We declare to you what was from the beginning, what we have heard, what we have seen with our eyes, what we have looked at and touched with our hands, concerning the word of life—this life was revealed, and we have seen it and testify to it, and declare to you the eternal life that was with the Father and was revealed to us.

All of life is sacred. When God reveals his heart to us, it will most likely come to us in the way described in 1 John. Did you notice? Heard with our ears, seen with our eyes, looked at and touched with our hands. We will know the presence of God through our five senses of hearing, seeing, touching, tasting and smelling. Dallas Willard says, "Human spiritual life always involves the use of our bodies. We have no other tools or instruments in the spiritual life than them."[25] It is through our physical senses that we are made alive to the kingdom of God. It is, for the family of humankind, our way of knowing.

> Fall in with the mood of the person to whom you are speaking. Be happy with those who are happy and sad with those who are sad. In a word, be all things to all men [women] so that you may gain all men.[26]

There is a three-way dynamic in spiritual mentoring that demands wholly listening by the mentor. Mentors must learn to become *trilingual* in their listening skills. They will listen (wholly), energetically, carefully and with concentration *to the mentoree,* their story and their needs. They will listen to what is *not* said, *how* things are said, *where* eyes dart or stare as stories are told. Second, the mentor will listen wholly *to the Holy Spirit,* whose voice may whisper quietly as the mentoree speaks. Is there a word the Spirit would like to give you for the mentoree, an insight into this person's life, a suggestion, a warning, an exercise of discipline for the week ahead? "Speak Lord, for your servant heareth." And third, wholly listening requires listening *to your own heart and instincts* as mentor. What is stirred within you, what creates consonance and where is dissonance? What part of you responds to the mentoree's story—reason, imagination, memory? How are you engaged by what you hear? When wholly listening is practiced, then holy listening occurs.

Reflection on the Practice of Jesus
In Mark 3 there is a description of an essential rhythm in Jesus' life.

> [Jesus] went up the mountain and called to him those whom he wanted, and they came to him . . . to be with him, and to be sent out. (Mk 3:13-14)

Jesus moved away from the busyness of his active life, taking with him certain ones "to be with him" and "to be sent out." It might be helpfully categorized as the journey apart, the journey within and the journey outward, for Jesus as mentor first moved away to create a place for them to be and from which they could be sent out. They moved apart in order to be. And then they were sent out until it was time again for them to move apart once more. It is an oft-repeated movement in Jesus' ministry of teaching his disciples.

In the high priestly prayer of John 14—16 we observe Jesus at work as spiritual mentor for his own disciples, the church. His movement toward the Father in prayer is suggestive of ways we can understand and practice spiritual mentoring.

For Reflection
Reflect on the ways that Jesus practices caring for his church. Consider how Jesus' prayer might guide the mentoring process in practical ways.

In John 14:1-10 Jesus guides his disciples to the Father. Even the words he speaks, says Jesus, are not his own; they are grounded in the heart of a Father whose intimate love for them has gone so far as to prepare a dwelling place for them. He understands spirituality as response to the already active presence of God. He listens.

In John 14:15-17 he points them to the Holy Spirit. The Paraclete

(Advocate or Helper) will come alongside to "abide with you" and to "be in you." It is a passage revealing selflessness on Jesus' part as he guides to the Father and points away from himself toward the work and ministry of the Holy Spirit. In John 16:13-14 he teaches that the Holy Spirit will complete the circle, and "he will glorify me, because he will take what is mine and declare it to you." Again, he draws the disciples to notice God's already active presence in the work of the Holy Spirit.

In John 14:1-3 and 14:27 he encourages them with hope for tomorrow. Attention to the future saturates this passage, not merely because Jesus will soon leave his disciples but because he insists that they understand the ongoing nature of their work and their need for relationship with the living God. They must attend to the present moment but always with an eye on the future.

In John 15:18 and 16:1-4, 32-33 he speaks honestly of the messiness of the real world. This is no wide-eyed idealist or sentimental optimist but one who is in touch with the grit and messiness of a world of rejection, persecution, desolation and struggle. Soon after these words were given to his friends, Jesus was arrested and faced all that he had just predicted. Jesus confronts the truth of the real world and insists that his disciples do so also. There is a reason for hope: God will transform the world and give peace and power. There is a reason for pain: the world in which we live is broken by sin and has no love lost for those who follow Jesus. He wanted his disciples to be ready to face whatever assaults would come.

In John 16:8 Jesus tells the truth about the human heart. Part of the reason we so urgently need to know the Holy Spirit is that we are capable of self-deception, self-defense and self-justification. Jesus told his disciples that the Holy Spirit will "prove the world wrong about sin and righteousness and judgement," and in 16:13 he promises that "when the Spirit of truth comes, he will guide you into all the truth." Mentoring is about truth telling, for truth is foundational to spiritual maturity.

In John 16:13 Jesus creates readiness for the already present activity of the Holy Spirit. Jesus intends for his disciples to know the heart and mind of the Holy Spirit. "I still have many things to say to you, but you cannot bear them now" (16:12). He encourages openness, readiness and anticipation to learn the next word from God.

Beginning in John 17:1 Jesus practices the ministry of prayer for his followers. "Holy Father, protect them in your name that you have given me, so that they may be one, as we are one" (17:11). In his absence from them, he prays for their protection, sanctification, unity and salvation. His attention to their spiritual growth does not end when their time together is over but continues onward through prayer.

Further Reflection for the Mentor

1. Create a setting in which your relationship with the mentoree can be comfortable and natural. There is no formula for how to begin each session together or how best to proceed, but it is important that you give direction for the process of establishing trust and intimacy—the fertile soil for the mentoring relationship.

2. It is essential that you don't use this time to dominate conversation with your latest spiritual insights, theological discoveries or personal issues. Remember this time is for the mentoree. The key is learning when to speak and when to listen.

3. Listen with your spiritual ear to the music of God's Holy Spirit who has brought you and the mentoree together. If you remember that this is God's business, you will remember to attend to God's agenda for the other. Yours is to listen to the music of the Holy Spirit. Prepare your mentoree in prayer.

Further Reflection for the Mentoree

1. Prepare yourself with prayer before you meet. The agenda for your time belongs to God. Ask God to help you prepare to listen. What can you do to nurture a meditative heart?

2. Prepare yourself by adjusting your expectations to the work of creatively listening to God. If you arrive expecting answers to questions, solutions to problems, advice to issues, you may miss the music God wants to teach your soul to sing.

3. Prepare by actively praying for your mentor as this person will pray for you.

Five

The Spirit of Teachability
Responsiveness

Blessed are those who hunger and thirst for righteousness.

JESUS

Those who are being mentored could begin to believe by now that the major work of mentoring is to be done by someone else to them as mentorees. Nothing could be further from the truth. The mentoree plays an active and involved role in the process of mentoring. The mentor takes the active role in creating a space, setting the times and structure in the mentoring relationship and giving shape to the conversation at hand. However, the mentoree is equally active in different and specific ways, which we call collectively *responsiveness*. Mentoring is a mutual process actively involving both mentor and mentoree.

This chapter will reflect on the role of the mentoree as active learner and "co-mentor," participant and agent in his or her own spiritual formation. Teachability, responsiveness and an open heart and mind—these are the essential modes of active learning for the mentoree. Two major themes will be discussed in this chapter, both of which are dimensions of the dynamic we call *responsiveness*.

First, what is my part as an active participant in the mentoring process? As a motivated and ready learner, what role do I play in my own spiritual growth? Teresa of Ávila will give us wise counsel and show us a way to assess our spiritual readiness.

Second, what happens when I face the difficult times of spiritual dryness when nourishment for my spirit seems only a distant memory or when I face the "dark nights of the soul" when God seems to have abandoned me to doubts, silence or spiritual emptiness? John of the Cross will describe the experience in his famous image of "dark night of the soul," as well as give wise advice on taking next steps toward ongoing spiritual responsiveness.

Responsiveness to the mentor is initially an act of willingness to listen on the part of the mentoree. This act is characterized by welcoming the mentor into the mentoree's life and making continuing choices for teachability. Hardly a passive role, responsiveness by the mentoree requires continual choices for readiness to learn. All students know that they can effectively handicap the teacher by their unwillingness to listen or their choice to be distracted from the process of learning. The role of the spiritual mentor is often to "facilitate (suggest, explain, motivate toward self-discovery) rather than command. . . . In other words, the drive for advancement must come from the mentoree."[1] According to Clinton, "Responsiveness describes the attitude of voluntary submission that a mentoree exhibits toward the mentor so that advice and assignments will be respected, appreciated, heeded and fulfilled."[2]

Many today are uncomfortable with the language of submission to another. In our era of democratized values, we may see any form of submission as inherently dangerous to the freedom of the self. Submissiveness, however, need not mean subservience or servility; rather submissiveness can refer to a spirit of readiness for learning, teachability and a responsive heart. Mentoring requires a willingness to listen for the wisdom embodied in the voices of mentors, contemporary or historical. Listening itself requires a posture of waiting and a readiness to hear another speak. This posture of attentive listening to the wisdom or direction of the mentor is an active choice for participation in mentoring by the mentoree. This dynamic of voluntary submission on the part of the mentoree raises questions such as, How do I become a responsive mentoree? How can I as a mentor affect a mentoree's responsiveness level? Questions like the following guide the process:

☐ What level of trust do I have in the mentor?

☐ How vulnerable am I prepared to be with my mentor?

☐ Do I thirst for "something more" in my spiritual journey?

☐ Am I willing to follow the insights and directives of another?

☐ Can I respect and love my mentor?

☐ Am I honest with myself when asked to look deep within?

☐ Can I be faithful to this type of mentoring relationship?

☐ What keeps me from submitting to the authority of another?

The Prelude to Growth

The prelude to the grand concert of spiritual growth begins when the mentoree answers questions about responsiveness like those listed above. Just as an orchestra warms up in anticipation of the leadership of the conductor, so the mentoree creates a teachable, ready spirit in preparation for the meetings with the mentor. What the mentoree brings by way of readiness and teachability will contribute directly to the effectiveness of the mentoring relationship. The prelude to growth sometimes includes the mentoree's stuttering questions and answers about readiness.

☐ Who is ready to be taught when learning may require a confrontation with a lifetime of habits, patterns and familiar answers?

☐ Who is ready to be taught when learning will certainly demand a challenge to self-deceptive sentimentality?

☐ Who is ready to be taught when learning will threaten that which is superficial, easy or inconsistent in my life?

The kind of learning required in spiritual mentoring may involve just such a confrontation with values, habits and styles of life. Readiness is neither automatic nor easy. Readiness to learn requires the preparation of prayer for ears willing to listen without defensiveness and a heart that is open for possible change. In some measure the answers to readiness questions are given in the prelude to the concert when we tune heart and will together. We often fail to understand that the discipline of the warm-up will often determine the quality of the concert. Without preparation there will be no grand concert performance! Without a teachable heart, responsive and ready to learn, there will be little growth. Responsiveness is an active work of the mentoree, prior to meetings with the mentor as well as during the meetings. Active participation by the mentoree begins with a spiritual warm-up through prayer for a willingness to learn and the courage to be responsive. Paradoxically, the more we become disciplined in the warm-up time, the freer and less bound we will be when the conductor begins to direct. We are desperate to become all that we can be and to become fully ourselves. Neither will happen until we submit to the spiritual discipline of responsiveness, for there are many factors, external and internal, that may hinder our readiness for spiritual formation.

The mentoree must also remember that submissiveness to the process of spiritual mentoring is primarily a submissiveness to the Holy Spirit, not a wooden, mindless obedience to a mentor. The mentor is a voice that guides but not a voice that dictates. Always the mentoree remains actively involved as agent within the context of sensitive listening. Without a spirit of submissiveness, change will remain an elusive longing. It is the role of the mentor to help us attend to the conditions of our life as they presently exist. The laboratory for the mentor will never be antiseptic but will always be cluttered with the earthly conditions of human life, things like family, relationships, conflicts, sin and physical health.

For Reflection
☐ Am I ready to learn and to submit to the guidance and innovations of my mentor?
☐ Do I hunger and thirst after righteousness enough to seek it with my whole heart and will?
☐ Am I willing to listen, ready to learn, open for transformation?
☐ Do I have a ready spirit of attentiveness that is willing to be engaged for my growth?

Teresa of Ávila and John of the Cross
Spiritual formation will take us ever more deeply into a respect for our imperfect human selves and into an ongoing relationship with the God who created us. Two voices from the sixteenth century will help us understand this discovery process.

Two of the most influential voices for our understanding and practice of spiritual mentoring are Teresa of Ávila (1515-1582) and John of the Cross (1542-1591). Through the last five centuries these two have invited people to a life of prayer that cultivates the soil of our souls and creates responsiveness. Their perspectives come to us not only from their own experiences as spiritual guides but also from their own mentoring relationship with one another. Teresa of Ávila and John of the Cross have influenced Christian spirituality by helping us understand the mysteries of the faith journey and the importance of responsiveness in unlocking those mysteries. They are included together because at different times each was a spiritual guide to the other.

Perhaps no other historical writer on spirituality has had such a widespread influence on people's experience of spiritual receptiveness as Teresa of Ávila. Teresa de Cepeda y Ahumada was born in 1515 to a wealthy family in Castile in Spain. In 1536 she entered a Carmelite convent, and in 1562 she founded the first discalced (barefoot) Carmelites, who practiced a more strict form of monastic life. Teresa arrived on the scene in the history of the church in the throes of transition and upheaval, which influenced the substance of her writings. In the maelstrom of change in the church that we call the Reformation, Teresa found herself leading a religious order and writing. Much to her own surprise, she discovered that her writings were helpful to others for the preparation of their openness to the spiritual experience.

Teresa's *The Way of Perfection* was written as a kind of manual to encourage a life of prayer among the nuns at St. Joseph's monastery. This work uplifted and supported the value of women in the church at a time when women were not given the same privilege of leadership in the church as were men. As Kavanaugh states, "This was the skeptical environment in which Teresa founded a monastery of women who dedicated themselves to a life of prayer, of intimate friendship with God, of living faith and love."[3] Like Aelred, Teresa understood prayer as "an intimate sharing between friends" for which one must frequently take time in order "to be alone with Him who we know loves us."[4] At the insistence of her own spiritual director, Father Gratian, she wrote another work, *Dwelling Places*. A few years later, in 1580, she wrote *The Interior Castle*, regarded as the best synthesis of her thoughts on spirituality. Teresa seemed to have a special interest in helping spiritual pilgrims learn how to create readiness for learning, listening and praying through her vital images and metaphors.

Teresa of Ávila was sought out as a spiritual mentor by many who desired a deeper sense of God's reality in their lives. Ironically, she was even sought out by the male leaders who were certain that a woman's place was not one of influence in the church. Early in her work Teresa was given the opportunity to become the mentor of a young friar named John. In a beautiful moment of historical irony, John would eventually become Teresa's spiritual director later in her life.

In 1568 John of the Cross became the chaplain of a new order of the Carmelites for friars, under the spiritual direction of Teresa. Alan Jones makes this comment about the tenacity of these two individuals:

It was in the face of bitter hardship and continual struggle against almost inconceivable pressures of ecclesiastical and political intrigue that they attained to a height of sanctity seldom paralleled in Christian history. Their dedication, their endurance and their unremitting love are their credentials as guides to Christians in all walks of life.[5]

Their two voices struggled to reestablish the values of spiritual formation at a time when the church fell prey to ecclesiastical and political power struggles. Their pathways were cluttered with political debris, social litter and ecclesiastical wreckage. Out of this turmoil emerged a most important insight: spiritual responsiveness requires the step of purgation or purification. John understood that intellect, memory and will are all faculties of the soul and that the instruction of each requires a step of purification. In *The Ascent of Mount Carmel* he states, "The same has to be done for the other two faculties, memory and will. They must undergo a purification relative to their respective apprehensions in order to reach union with God in perfect hope and charity."[6] John sees the need for a process of purification that goes much deeper than the familiar psychobabble of "owning" your feelings or memories. We might most easily think of purification as a process of clearing the pathway.

Clearing the pathway of impediments will always remain a lively and necessary spiritual practice. The prophetic voice of John the Baptist said, "I am the voice of one crying out in the wilderness, 'Make straight the way of the Lord.'" In the ancient world a servant would precede the advent of royalty by running ahead to clear the road of debris or obstructions, thus making the pathway safe for those who followed. The metaphors of debris and the road are significant. To get on the road means you have to clear the path of debris. John's message was for responsiveness: "Get ready for the coming of the Lord."

What is the debris to be cleared from your life in preparation for the coming of the Lord? *Debris* might refer to those things in the past that get in your way. Debris is something that you dropped here last time, something that blew into your way last time, something that you keep carrying along with you that causes you to trip. It may be guilt, memories, old habits, an old self-image, old dreams or old ways of thinking. Any of these things may obstruct your clear passage on the road to spiritual maturity. There are also present distractions, barriers that slow you down or stop you from continuing on the way or burdens in your life that are too heavy or too clumsy to allow you to stay on the way. There may be detours. These are misdirections that take you off the pathway and take you away from the destination. John the Baptist says to us that he has come to clear that debris, remove those distractions and help us avoid those detours. How does that happen? Responsiveness requires purification of the heart. Teresa talks about this step as the work of "courageous souls."

Courageous Souls

Teresa came to believe from her own experience that God is drawn to those who hunger and thirst for righteousness, who are, in other words, not content with little. What we have called "a longing for more" Teresa understood as the courage of the soul to desire God more and more and to persevere in the search to know God. In her various writings she said God was "emphatically 'a friend of courageous souls,' a God who truly wants this determination."[7] She said insistently that God does not "deny Himself to anyone who perseveres."[8]

Courageous souls are those with an intensity of desire, determination, discipline and persistence. Teresa seemed to see a causal relationship between discipline and deepened desire, for she said to the women under her leadership,

> The more she learns about the greatness of her God . . . the more her desire increases. For the more is revealed to her of how much this great God and Lord deserves to be loved, the more does her love for him grow. . . . His Majesty has the power to do all that He wishes and He is desirous of doing a great deal for us.[9]

Jesus said it simply, "Blessed are those who hunger and thirst for righteousness" (Mt 5:6). The receptive heart is the hungry heart. Today we seek to satisfy our hunger through spiritual fast foods that lack nourishment for the soul. Teresa's passion was for the single-mindedness of heart that aggressively hungers to know God and thus to be loved by God.

Three steps are essential for the insistent determination that Teresa believed makes us receptive and responsive for spiritual formation.

The first is knowledge of the greatness of God: the more we see of this, the more deeply we are conscious of it. The second is self-knowledge and humility at realizing how a thing like the soul, so base by comparison with One Who is the Creator of such greatness, has dared to offend Him and dares to raise its eyes to Him. The third is a supreme contempt for earthly things, save those which can be employed in the service of so great a God.[10]

To know God, to know the self, to submit with eyes open to the dangers of the world—these three make us receptive for spiritual formation. The focus is on the self but through the lens of a prior focus on the greatness God in the context of a focus on the world. Her three-part process mirrors Jesus' prayer for his disciples. First, we acknowledge our Father, the sovereign in heaven—revere God's name and acknowledge the priority of his kingdom. Second, we ask forgiveness for our sins, and third, we seek protection from the earthly things that might lead us astray.

When we focus on God we recognize our serious need for a purified heart. When Isaiah walked into the temple in his mystical vision in Isaiah 6, he became aware of the majesty of God. "I saw the Lord sitting on a throne, high and lofty" (v. 1). The almost immediate result was a profound awareness of his need for a purified heart. "And I said: 'Woe is me! I am lost, for I am a man of unclean lips, and I live among a people of unclean lips; yet my eyes have seen the King, the LORD of hosts!' " (v. 5).

When Isaiah's vision was filled with the holiness, purity and majesty of God, his response focused on his own need for cleansing. This is the process we call responsiveness in this chapter, for we create a receptive heart through such purification of the soul; we clear away the debris of sin, rebellion, selfishness, disobedience and failure.

It is the nearly universal contention of classical spiritual writers that we need to confront the profound reality of our sinfulness. This is not a popular concept in the church today, but we ignore it only at great risk to our spiritual formation. To deny our sinfulness is surely a sham in a world of such obvious human sin. To ignore our need for purification is the worst kind of personal self-deception. The apostle Paul would strongly agree, for he wrote of the two steps necessary for spiritual formation in Colossians, that great treatise on spiritual growth. In Colossians 3:5-11 he speaks in specific detail of this step of purification:

Put to death, therefore, whatever in you is earthly: fornication, impurity, passion, evil desire, and greed (which is idolatry). On account of these the wrath of God is coming on those who are disobedient. These are the ways you also once followed, when you were living that life. But now you must get rid of all such things—anger, wrath, malice, slander, and abusive language from your mouth. Do not lie to one another, seeing that you have stripped off the old self with its practices and have clothed yourselves with the new self, which is being renewed in knowledge according to the image of its creator. In that renewal there is no longer Greek and Jew, circumcised and uncircumcised, barbarian, Scythian, slave and free; but Christ is all in all!

The step of negation or purgation is followed quickly in Colossians 3:12-15 with words of affirmation and positive assent:

As God's chosen ones, holy and beloved, clothe yourselves with compassion, kindness, humility, meekness, and patience. Bear with one another and, if anyone has a complaint against another, forgive each other; just as the Lord has forgiven you, so you must also forgive. Above all, clothe yourselves with love, which binds everything together in perfect harmony. And let the peace of Christ rule in your hearts, to which indeed you were called in the one body.

For centuries the practice of the church has included the daily discipline of reading the psalms. Saturated in the psalms we become saturated with the greatness of God, aware of God's otherness, power, majesty, glory, creativity, beauty, singular authority, constancy, grace, justice and compassion. Before this God we can only echo the response of Teresa by becoming humble and reorienting our values to focus on the things of the Lord.

Much spiritual self-help today fails because the focus remains exclusively on the self: How can *I* grow? How can *I* experience God more fully? How can *I* access the power of the Holy Spirit? How can *I* develop *my* faith? All of these are limited questions that lead to disappointment because they do not focus on God. The unison voice of the classical spiritual teachers recounts that spiritual growth always begins with an awareness of the character and nature of God. God starts the process; we respond. God initiates; we act. God speaks; we answer. Teresa wanted her apprentices to sustain a vision of God's greatness. Through our focus on God, we can then look at the self and the world, which so easily distract us.

Today we tend to mistrust anything that negates the value, rights and sanctity of the human ego. The human self has become deified in Western culture to the point that many will reject Teresa's wisdom outright. "She speaks so negatively of the 'baseness' of the human person and with such contempt for the culture in which we live, why should we respect her words?" Teresa understood that spiritual formation must take consideration of the earthly context in which people live. Her own life and times introduced her to the oppression and harshness of political, social and ecclesiastical systems that had lost sight of the greatness of God. She wrote not from the security of middle-class comfort but from an embattled political system that sometimes denigrated the leadership of its women. Her words are grounded in the harsh realities of her time, but she views these realities through the lens of a deeply biblical understanding of historic Christian doctrines of God, sin and the world. Do you remember our letter to mentors and mentorees in chapter one in which we spoke about three movements toward spiritual growth? In it we listed three essential questions: Who is God? Who am I? What am I called to do?

For Reflection

☐ What in your past has helped to make you receptive, teachable and responsive to the teaching of another?

☐ What practical steps have you already found to be effective in creating a heart of readiness to listen and to learn?

☐ What keeps you from having an open heart?

☐ What debris in your life clutters the pathway, preventing your responsiveness and hindering your progress?

Journey of the Interior Castle

In 1970 Pope Paul IV named Teresa a Doctor of the Church, in part because of her descriptive writings of her own theophanies and moments of epiphany. She had what has been called a "second conversion," which came through visions of Christ. These visions and her ensuing spiritual journey led her to establish Carmelite houses for the spiritual practice of contemplation. Her grandest written work is *The Interior Castle*, which describes seven *moradas*, dwelling places or mansions for believers. The closer one moves to the seventh mansion, the closer one is to God. She presents these not as seven steps for mentors to follow but rather as a description of her own mystical experience with God. She does, however, invite all of her spiritual daughters to enter their own "interior castle" because, she believed, such an experience with God was possible for all. Some see *The Interior Castle* as a mystical account of raptures and ecstatic visions available to only the most advanced spiritual persons. We cite one translator of her work who disagrees:

> She intended it for the instruction of her own daughters and of all other souls, who, either in her own day or later, might have the ambition to penetrate either the outer or the inner Mansions. At all times in the history of Christian perfection there has been a dearth of persons qualified to guide souls to the highest states of prayer: *The Interior Castle* will both serve as an aid to those there are and to a great extent supply the need for more.[11]

Reading *The Interior Castle* is like listening to a Mozart composition after playing pop music on the radio en route to Orchestra Hall. After hearing the depth, complexity and beauty of Mozart, you comprehend the shallow superficiality of the music to which your ears have become attuned. The music of pop culture is enlarged, the small horizon is expanded to the farthest point, and the limited musical vocabulary of simplistic sound is deepened by the richness of music that has lasted for centuries.

Teresa's musical vocabulary is not the limited lexicon of Christian pop culture. Teresa understood the development of the soul as multilayered and richly textured. *The Interior Castle* is a passionate work written to instruct her beloved sisters, a work that grew from her own vision of God's desire for the soul, words rich in the music of the soul.

> I began to think of the soul as if it were a castle made of a single diamond or of very clear crystal, in which there are many rooms, just as in Heaven there are many mansions.... I can find nothing with which to compare the great beauty of the soul and its great capacity.[12]

The first mansion Teresa describes is where most people live. Although they sense there is more to life, they are busy and focus their energy on the mundane issues of life and death. In this chapter Teresa acknowledges the dignity of the human soul, made in the image and likeness of God, but observes that most people are content to live in the shadow of spiritual depth.

The residents of mansion two have progressed enough to learn a life of prayer and have developed an increased sense of awareness of God through sermons, books and friendships. Those who have moved into mansion two have begun progress toward something more.

In mansion three people are learning daily to become more sensitized to God's presence and show some charity toward others, but they are limited in their acts of benevolence. The residents here exhibit a high standard of virtue, but this virtue has not yet learned self-surrender or selfless love.

Teresa said, "The important thing is not to think much but to love much."[13] Those in mansion four have learned to move beyond thinking about faith or doing religious activities to a deeper understanding of faith motivated by love. They realize their need for the supernatural in their lives. No longer content or able to serve in their own strength, they seek ever increasingly to pay attention to the presence of God's power for life.

In the fifth mansion the soul approaches God. As the silkworm dies within the cocoon and a beautiful white butterfly emerges from death, even so the soul is transformed. In this way, Teresa sees the soul preparing to receive the gift of God's presence.

The sixth mansion is a place of much tribulation as the person, like an engaged person, now betrothed to Jesus, prepares for union with him in totality. The person experiences increasing intimacy accompanied by increasing afflictions.

The final mansion is the place of the soul's marriage to Christ, for as Paul said, "For to me, living is Christ and dying is gain" (Phil 1:21). In this mansion of the King the believer experiences complete transformation.

Teresa's obvious goal was marriage to Christ, union with him, oneness with the Lord. But such union with Christ is not merely a spiritual reality; it is lived in service and labor for the kingdom. Two quotations will suffice.

> This, my sisters, I should like us to strive to attain: we should desire and engage in prayer, not for our enjoyment, but for the sake of acquiring this strength which fits us for service.[14]
>
> Fix your eyes on the Crucified and nothing else will be of much importance to you. If His Majesty revealed His love to us by doing and

suffering such amazing things, how can you expect to please Him by words alone? Do you know when people really become spiritual? It is when they become the slaves of God and are branded with His sign, which is the sign of the Cross, in token that they have given Him their freedom.[15]

Teresa's seven mansions guide us to understand more richly the ways to deepen our responsiveness as mentorees. The allegory describes seven movements of prayer and can be used as a very practical guide to assess spiritual progress toward deeper intimacy with God. There are some very practical uses for this work: The mentor might choose to use Teresa's seven mansions as a guide to assist the mentoree in progressing from superficial prayer to the deepest, most intimate prayer of mystical union with Christ. The mentoree might choose to study Teresa's modes of prayer to learn new ways to deepen responsiveness, ways to advance in spiritual growth. A mentoree will not experience a linear, sequential growth through each of these seven mansions as if they are steps on a ladder for spiritual formation. Rather the mansions form a stable vantage point from which we can stand to view the meandering steps of our pilgrimage. Finally, the mentor might use the seven mansions as a way to invite the mentoree to assess his or her level of spiritual maturity.

Journey of the Dark Night
Juan de Yepes y Alvarez was born in 1542 in Fontiveros, Spain, only twenty-four miles from the birthplace of Teresa of Ávila. He was raised by his poor widowed mother and attended a school for poor and orphaned children. John received his higher education in the disciplines of grammar, rhetoric, Greek, Latin and religion from the Jesuit College from 1559 to 1563. He knew God had called him to a religious order as a way of life, and in 1563, at the age of twenty, he entered a Carmelite Order. Being a gifted thinker, John soon thereafter continued his education at the University of Salamanca, a school comparable to the University of Paris or Oxford.

In 1567 John met Teresa of Ávila for the first time in his hometown of Medina del Campo. John was recommended to Teresa as the one who could help her launch a contemplative community for friars of the Carmelite Order. John had desired such a life and ministry and agreed to be the confessor and chaplain of this new community. Teresa became his spiritual mentor for the new life and ministry John was to begin. He took for himself the name John of the Cross because of the intense suffering he experienced in his life.

Teresa saw great leadership potential in young John and put him in charge of the order. During his lifetime John established several Carmelite orders of a similar nature throughout Spain. He was known as a contemplative, theologian, poet, reformer and administrator, but one of his most prominent ministries was his role as spiritual director to many of his students and to people of high position who sought out his holy wisdom. John of the Cross held firmly the conviction that in order to reach one's potential as a human being, one needed to strive to encounter intimacy with God, a striving that became a primary focus of his mentoring relationships. He was especially concerned with teaching souls "the dynamics of growth in union with God."[16]

John's was a model life lived to the fullest in devout love and service to God. He was eventually imprisoned by those who opposed his work for reform in the churches and monasteries of the day. He suffered greatly in prison at the hands of leaders in the church who found his ideals to be damaging to their power and authority. He was placed in solitude for long periods of time and was cruelly mistreated during his imprisonment. John of the Cross died at the age of forty-nine on December 13, 1591.

Like Teresa of Ávila, John lived as mystic and prophet-reformer.

> He withdrew from the world to be close to God, yet the doorway to God was through the wonder of nature and human love. He was blinded into a loving darkness by the brightness of the Sun. What he saw left him stunned and stammering. His response to the wonder of the dazzling darkness was to write love poems. He wrote his greatest ones in the midst of terrible suffering. He was tortured and crippled by his accusers (members of his own community!), yet he wrote joyfully and without rancor. He was severe against himself. He bore no resentment.[17]

As Teresa's friend and advocate, John was imprisoned in an unlit cell where he suffered severe pain from the bitter cold and stifling heat of the prison. Even in the worst moments of his suffering, like the apostle Paul, John of the Cross found a spiritual ability to write passionate poetry to God and to give voice to his wonder at the rapturous beauty of God.

During his periods of confinement, he wrote *The Dark Night of the Soul.*

It describes God's work in the life of a believer through sorrow, suffering and darkness. The phrase is used somewhat broadly by people, often without an understanding of the profound meaning of John's significant teaching. The "dark night" is that time when people lose the joy they once experienced in their spiritual disciplines and faith practices. John taught that this happens because God wants to purify their souls and move them to deeper faith. In the beginning of faith, God will move gently in a person's life, like a mother with an infant, seeking to nurture and care for the child. As time proceeds, however, there comes a time for the child to grow into adulthood, and God invites them to grow through the experience of the dark night of the soul. The perceived darkness is that time when God appears to withdraw from the individual. It is often a time of intense difficulty as the person of faith undergoes the loss of the sense of God's active presence. The reward is purification of the soul that furthers faith development.

John's writings are demanding and complex as they take us through the times of spiritual dryness, spiritual shadows and spiritual struggle. The work of spiritual mentoring will often require interaction with a mentoree in the midst of such a dark night of the soul. John wanted to provide for his mentorees a sense of courage as they together journeyed through the dark night of the soul. The mentor needed obvious ability in the task of guiding someone through the experience of the dark night.

For John of the Cross, the Christian journey of faith was a journey initiated by the decision to die to oneself, thereby discovering the essence of existence as a loved child of God. Such a journey was not an easy one. It demanded a stripping away of that which motivates the self in order to be united with God and desire him only. This journey of the dark night toward intimacy with God through prayer has two distinct movements: (1) the active night, which involves proactive prayerful disciplines practiced by the mentoree, and (2) the passive night, which is initiated by God in the life of the responsive mentoree and requires a posture of responsive waiting by the mentoree.

Once in the passive night the mentoree is often perplexed by the shallowness of a prayer made up of words and enters a greater awareness of a relationship with God via passive contemplation. As the mentoree draws closer to God, frustration may set in because words, once adequate to describe the experience, are no longer valid. John of the Cross cites the philosopher Aristotle to describe the spiritual phenomenon of experiencing the "dark night."

The clearer and more obvious divine things are in themselves, the darker and more hidden they are to the soul naturally. The brighter the light the more the owl is blinded; and the more one looks at the brilliant sun, the more the sun darkens the faculty of sight, deprives it and overwhelms it in its weakness.[18]

As the responsive mentoree embarks on the journey of the dark night with its peculiar movements, the task of the spiritual mentor is to provide encouragement and motivation to continue the journey. Together, mentor and mentoree learn to pay attention to the blinding light of the Spirit in the life of the mentoree. John of the Cross clarifies the reason behind the "darkness" created from the Light:

Hence when the divine light of contemplation strikes souls not yet entirely illumined, it causes spiritual darkness, for it not only surpasses them but also deprives and darkens their act of understanding. This is why St. Dionysius and other mystical theologians call this infused contemplation a ray of darkness; that is, for the soul not yet illumined and purged. For this great supernatural light overwhelms the intellect and deprives it of its natural vigor.[19]

Thus the mentoree discovers that darkness is only a perception of God's absence and withdrawal. What appears to be dark is actually the blindness that comes as one draws closer to the light. Like a child who looks straight at the brilliance of the sun, the light creates a blindness to its brilliance. The sunshine that causes us to look away is analogous to the experience of drawing nearer to Christ. We are forced into the "darkness" of new questions, uncharted territory and a new deeper experience of God's presence that will eventually illuminate our lives once again. A mentor offers the best hope of seeing through the experience of the dark night into the experience of light once again.

John describes a mentor as one who possesses a discerning and listening spirit and provides motivation and inspiration. Teresa was mentor to John, who became mentor to Teresa. The historical particulars of their story show us the delicate interaction between mentor and mentoree. There are echoes of understanding in John that are directly responsive to the song that Teresa sang. Like Teresa, he believed the mentoree must carry a heart of readiness into the process of spiritual direction. Two important quotations clarify his thought:

> Oh, if people knew how much spiritual good and abundance they lose by not attempting to raise their appetites above childish things, and if they knew to what extent, by not desiring the taste of these trifles, they would discover in this simple spiritual food the savor of them all![20]
>
> Anyone desiring to climb to the summit of the mount in order to become an altar for the offering of a sacrifice of pure love and praise and reverence to God, must first accomplish these three tasks perfectly.
>
> First, he must cast out the strange gods, all alien affections and attachments.
>
> Second, through a habitual denial and repentance of these appetites—by the dark night of the senses—he must purify himself of their residue.
>
> The third requisite for reaching the top of this high mount is the change of garments.[21]

John of the Cross practiced a spiritual mentoring that understood the main active character in the relationship as the already active presence of God, through the Holy Spirit, who eventually revealed God's love and desired will in the life of the mentoree. This unique relationship fostered a depth of intimacy with God necessary for the mentoree's journey of faith and growing awareness and maturity of self.

How then do we use this material? At first glance we might be overwhelmed by its complexity and depth. Are there practical uses of the material that came from lives of contemplation and spiritual ecstasy? What can I draw from the writing of John of the Cross? How do I use John's model? From the beginning, this chapter has tried to create this principle: if I want to grow into intimacy with God through the process of spiritual mentoring, I will need to learn how to become more submissive. If growth is my heart's desire I will ask, "How will the mentor direct me?" My role in the dynamic interaction of spiritual mentoring is to share most openly and honestly the stories and experiences of my journey. John of the Cross understood that there are beginners in faith and there are those whose maturity has been deepened by experience.

Entering the Dark Night of the Soul

Listen to a common complaint from a mentoree:

I'm meeting with my mentor, going through the various prayer exercises and spiritual disciplines. I find that Scripture doesn't mean what it used to, my prayers don't carry, I am praying more, reading more, doing more and I find less of God. It finally comes to a point when I can't pray any more because I don't know the words. I have run out of words to say to God.

John of the Cross would say to us that we are precisely where we should be—that now we are ready to enter the passive night where we really discover intimacy with God because we can see what God is doing for us, through us, in us. True prayer is about what God is doing for us, not about all that we are trying to do. The more we look at God, the darker our sight becomes because we are blinded by the purity of the God we worship. We are now in the dark night of the soul. But this darkness is not a place of failure and distance; rather it is a place of increasing intimacy with God. When as a child you watched someone weld, you were taught that if you looked at the intense light of the arc welder, it could blind you. John uses the metaphor of the natural light. If we look into the light of God's purity, we will come to a place where we see less, not more. The brightness creates darkened sight.

At this vulnerable moment the mentor must help the mentoree realize that growth is all around. The darker it becomes, the greater the potential for growth because this "dark night of the soul" has opened us to the darkness of our own spiritual abilities. When Moses got close to the light of the burning bush, he turned away, "hid his face," because he was afraid. The more intimately he knew God, the more Moses experienced darkness, a darkness of fear, confusion, anxious wondering. It is the paradox of the dark night. Greater maturity is born in the purgation of the dark night.

The time of darkness is not a period of punishment or distance but a movement to greater depth in prayer in which the mentoree moves toward intimacy with God. Responsiveness is all about the mentoree's desire to grow toward God. The teachings of John of the Cross help us know what will happen as we move deeper in that relationship. The wise mentor will help the mentoree understand that God is working to deepen the level of love. As one journeys closer to God, one enters this phase of darkness, which is the purgation, the dying to oneself, which will actually reveal life, as Jesus teaches us in Matthew 10:39, "Those who find their life will lose it, and those who lose their life for my sake will find it."

Prayer is a pilgrimage. The closer I get to the goal, the farther away I might feel. The more holy I become, the less holy I know myself to be. The more experienced I am in my ministry, the less competent I may feel to lead others to spiritual growth. Is this merely a loss of confidence, or is it part of the pilgrimage to spiritual maturity? John's writings help us discern our progress to spiritual maturity.

The birth process, for the child being born, is actually an experience of death to the life he or she knows. The child is swimming in a warm, familiar and nurturing place of gentleness and care. Suddenly, the infant is wrenched from the place of nurture into a cold, dark place that feels constricted, narrow, limiting and harsh. The violence of the birth process begins the moment the child is wrenched from the womb into the birth canal. On the other side will be light, warmth, nurture and care, but the painful passage requires time in the dark of the birth canal. The dark night experience of spiritual passage resembles the unpleasant and difficult experience in the birth canal. John writes,

> I should not like to persuade spiritual persons that the road leading to God does not entail a multiplicity of considerations, methods, manners and experiences—though in their own way these may be requirements for beginners—but demands only the one thing necessary: true self-denial, exterior and interior, through surrender of self both to suffering for Christ and to annihilation in all things. . . . A man makes progress only through imitation of Christ, Who is the Way, the Truth, and the Life. . . . Accordingly, I should not consider any spirituality worthwhile that would walk in sweetness and ease and run from the imitation of Christ.[22]

The work of John of the Cross is especially pertinent in the atmosphere of the commercialized marketplace of spirituality today, which "sells" certain forms of prayer (for example, prayers of the desert fathers, contemplative prayer, transcendental meditation) as more highly spiritual than others. John believed prayer to be the basic communication for those who are ever seeking to grow in their experience of God. He taught that contemplative prayer, for example, belongs to the life of ordinary Christians: "There is no state of prayer so exalted that it will not be necessary to return to the beginnings."[23] Across the centuries true believers have experienced the dark night of the soul; today we are told to avoid pain at all costs. John sought to normalize the experience of darkness as a necessary step toward maturity; today we seek to anesthetize any experiences that are unpleasant, confusing, painful or shadowy.

A Primer for the Disciplines of the Soul

In *The Dark Night* John of the Cross gives a fascinating list of "imperfections commonly found in beginners," a kind of compendium of warnings for us all on the journey of spiritual growth. In the spirit of Helmut Thielicke's small book *Exercises to Young Theologians,* John's list challenges and warns young mentors, young teachers, young pastors, young disciples and all of us in the early steps of our spiritual lives. We include them here because of their amazing contemporaneity. The mentoree will benefit from slowly studying and attending to these wise cautions for any who would undertake a serious plan for spiritual formation.

1. They develop spiritual pride.

    These beginners feel so fervent and diligent in their spiritual exercises and undertakings that a certain kind of secret pride is generated in them which begets a complacency with themselves and their accomplishments, despite the fact that holy works do of their very nature cause humility.[24]

2. They know more than they practice.

    Many never get enough of hearing counsels, or of learning spiritual maxims, or of keeping them and reading books about them. They spend more time doing this than striving after mortification and the perfection of the interior poverty to which they are obliged.[25]

3. Though spiritually motivated, their character remains unchanged.

    They become peevish in the works they do and easily angered by the least thing, and occasionally they are so unbearable that nobody can put up with them. This frequently occurs after they have experienced in prayer some recollection pleasant to the senses.[26]

4. They become spiritually superior and judgmental of others.

    Through a certain indiscreet zeal they become angry over the sins of others, they reprove these others, and sometimes even feel the impulse to do so angrily, which in fact they occasionally do, setting themselves up as lords of virtue.[27]

5. They are greedy for spiritual experience, rather than a knowledge of God.

    Many, lured by the delight and satisfaction procured in their relig-

ious practices, strive more for spiritual savor than for spiritual purity
and discretion, yet it is the purity and discretion which God looks
for and finds acceptable throughout a soul's entire spiritual journey.[28]

6. They deify the experience of God.

In communicating they spend all their time trying to get some
feeling and satisfaction rather than humbly praising and reverencing
God dwelling within them.[29]

In receiving Communion they spend all their time trying to get
some feeling and satisfaction rather than humbly praising and
reverencing God dwelling within them. And they go about this in
such a way that, if they do not procure any sensible feeling and
satisfaction, they think they have accomplished nothing. . . . Once
they do not find delight in prayer, or any other spiritual exercise, they
feel extreme reluctance and repugnance in returning to it and
sometimes even give it up. For after all . . . they are like children who
are prompted to act not by reason but by pleasure.[30]

7. They measure their spiritual progress by their experience.

They think the whole matter of prayer consists in looking for sensory
satisfaction and devotion. They strive to procure this by their own
efforts and tire and weary their heads and their faculties. When they
do not get this sensible comfort, they become very disconsolate and
think they have done nothing.[31]

8. They compete for spiritual progress with others.

In regard to envy, many of them will feel sad about the spiritual good
of others and experience sensible grief in noting that their neighbor
is ahead of them on the road to perfection, and they will not want
to hear others praised. . . . Their annoyance grows because they
themselves do not receive these plaudits and because they long for
preference in everything.[32]

9. They lack perseverance and grow weary of spiritual discipline.

[They] become weary in the more spiritual exercises and flee from them,
since these exercises are contrary to sensory satisfaction. Since they are
so used to finding delight in spiritual practices, they become bored when
they do not find it. . . . As a result they strive to satisfy their own will
rather than God's.[33]

10. They are unwilling to "count the cost."

Like those who are reared in luxury, they run sadly from everything rough, and they are scandalized by the cross, in which spiritual delights are found.[34]

For Reflection
☐ When have you experienced times of spiritual darkness, confusion or the absence of God?
☐ How have you understood these experiences?
☐ What helped you to grow through the times of darkness?

John was a spiritual mentor who lived in solitude much of the time and yet often called his Carmelite brothers to live in union with God. As we continually seek to experience God more fully, John of the Cross presses us never to settle for that which we can know but rather to seek that which we cannot comprehend. Rather than settle for the superficialities of pop spirituality today, John of the Cross would urge us onward into the depths of faith.

Since God is unapproachable and hidden . . . however much it seem to thee that thou findest and feelest and understandest him, thou must ever hold him as hidden and serve him after a hidden manner as one that is hidden.[35]

Receptivity in the Heart of the Mentoree
John of the Cross shared Teresa's sense of the receptive, courageous heart, though his language is more poetic and his mood more pensive.

To reach satisfaction in all
    desire its possession in nothing.
To come to possess all
    desire the possession of nothing.
To arrive at being all
    desire to be nothing.
To come to the knowledge of all
    desire the knowledge of nothing.
To come to the pleasure you have not
    you must go by a way in which you enjoy not.
To come to the knowledge you have not

you must go by a way in which you know not.
To come to the possession you have not
    you must go by a way in which you possess not.
To come to be that which you are not
    you must go by a way in which you are not.
When you turn toward something
    you cease to cast yourself upon the all.
For to go from all to the all
    you must deny yourself of all in all.
And when you come to the possession of the all
    you must possess it without wanting anything.
Because if you desire to have something in all
    your treasure in God is not purely your all.[36]

It is this spirit of readiness, alertness and hunger that will create the space for spiritual growth. And as always, John urges for all the assistance of a spiritual guide: "If there is no one to understand these persons, they either turn back and abandon the road or lose courage, or at least they hinder their own progress."[37]

What does the mentoree bring to the conversation? Receptivity of heart is a commonly repeated theme among the great writers of spiritual direction. They understood that spiritual mentoring does not consist of a program of activities imposed on another by a mentor, as a weight-training coach instructs an athlete; rather, spiritual mentoring is an interactive process that relies on the receptivity of the mentoree. A summary of essential mentoree characteristics is like musical notes that together create the melody of the soul:

☐ vulnerability in sharing intimate issues of life
☐ desire for spiritual growth and maturity
☐ responsiveness to directives of the mentor
☐ a respectful and loving attitude toward the mentor
☐ longing to serve God
☐ teachable spirit
☐ faithfulness to mentoring relationship, as well as other life responsibilities

Vulnerability means that the mentoree will intend and develop the practice of unmasking. "Saving face" is surely the greatest hindrance to spiritual growth in the process of spiritual mentoring.

Desire is hunger. Desire is thirst. Desire for spiritual growth and maturity is not a casual taste but a raging hunger and thirst. Jesus warned us to undertake spiritual surgery if the eye or hand offends. Such surgery does not seek a second opinion but looks to the interior of the self and determines to listen to the Great Physician.

Responsiveness to the direction of the mentor is the simple willingness to try what is suggested with an open and ready heart. Responsiveness requires submission. It may be the hardest thing for individualistic and self-determined Christians today! The spiritual direction of the past was a process of being directed, guided and led. There was authority in the relationship, although the best spiritual direction was typically nondirective as it emerged from the wisdom of the conversation.

Perhaps we are more comfortable today with the language of *respect* for the mentor, but most people who enter the conversation of mentoring will soon observe the development of love for the mentor, a gratitude and appreciation for the other. Such love cannot be forced and must not be seen as prerequisite for developing a relationship; it is instead a product of a relationship of mutual trust and vulnerability.

The *longing to serve* is a response to the great goodness and love of God. We do not serve in order to bargain with God, in order to earn God's favor, but as a joyful response to God's love. If the mentoree wishes for power for self, whether it is spiritual or otherwise, he or she is likely to be disappointed. Maturity means self-denial rather than self-enhancement. Maturity does not require the asceticism of spiritual rigorists who believed that we must deny or even crush the self through disciplines of self-flagellation; rather, the maturity we desire involves taking off the clothing of the fallen self as Paul describes in Colossians.

The spirit that is *teachable* is a ready spirit. Any classroom teacher with experience can sniff out a teachable spirit in minutes. Some with the facade of teachability have watched the videos and know to sit in the front, hair slicked back, notebook open, eyes bright and wide open, hand raised to ask questions even before class begins. The veteran teacher will know quickly enough whether there is a teachable spirit behind the facade. The teachable spirit brings one dominant quality into the classroom or mentoring conversation: attentiveness. Like the child with a hundred questions, the teachable mentoree arrives having spent the previous week in wide-eyed attention to life and to mentoring assignments and is patiently ready for more. Children are teachable precisely because they are so greedy for more knowledge and are unashamedly demanding in seeking what they want to know. They may be greedy for information, but often they are simply greedy to "know" in body, heart and soul.

Hindrances to Mentoring

1. Some people simply do not see their need for help. They are strong individualists or, at least, determinedly private in their faith and have never considered that someone else might be of assistance to their spiritual formation.

2. Some have little confidence that they are worthy of the time of another person, especially if they perceive the mentor to be important or busy. Their own feelings of inadequacy block them from seeking what may be the most important step they might take for their spiritual growth.

3. Many, we believe, live behind the façade of spiritual adequacy and competence. Afraid to let down the mask, they maintain a strong public image that greatly distorts their own interior pain, fear, weakness, inadequacy or history. Because they are already in positions of leadership or maturity, they believe they should have it all together and dare not show the weakness of seeking out a mentor.

4. Some have good reasons for refusing the ministry of mentoring: They have had poor experiences with teachers, coaches or mentors in the past. Their history of bad mentoring, hurtful relationships or even abuse at the hand of leaders creates a hesitation that hinders their involvement.

5. One roadblock to someone's being empowered through spiritual mentoring may be an unwillingness to submit to the authority of another. Not only does this impede the work of a mentor, but it also impedes the work of the Spirit. I can only understand what it means to be in a position of authority after I have learned what it means to be in a position of submission. Similarly, I can only learn what it means to function in spiritual authority after I have learned what it means to submit to the Spirit's work in my life. A mentoree who is unwilling to be submissive will also be unwilling to be responsive to the directives of the mentor.

Further Reflection for the Mentor

1. Have you carefully created a covenant with your mentoree?

2. How is your relationship growing in the soil of the mentoree's life, that

is, how have you tried to bring the conversation to reflection on the real, even messy parts of his or her life?

3. Are you continuing in prayer and growing in affection for the mentoree?

4. Consider your own hesitations or questions about mentoring: Is there something that might hinder you from seeking out a mentor or accepting a mentoring relationship with another?

Further Reflection for the Mentoree

1. Are you aware of hindrances to your responsiveness and teachability? Are you consciously alert to any barriers to your openness to work in this mentoring relationship with this mentor?

2. What can you do to increasingly unmask in order to become more vulnerable to the Holy Spirit?

3. How do you assess your teachability, responsiveness and readiness for spiritual guidance?

Six

Exercises of Grace
Accountability

Finally, be strong in the Lord and in the strength of his power.
Put on the whole armor of God, so that you may be able
to stand against the wiles of the devil. For our struggle is not against
enemies of blood and flesh, but against the rulers, against
the authorities, against the cosmic powers of this present darkness,
against the spiritual forces of evil in the heavenly places.
Therefore take up the whole armor of God, so that you may
be able to withstand on that evil day, and having done
everything, to stand firm.

THE APOSTLE PAUL

If the purpose of mentoring is to enable us to become more Christlike, we still have to ask, How is it done? What are practices or disciplines that will help us on the road to growth? Thomas R. Kelly, in his classic work *A Testament of Devotion*, says,

> Life is meant to be lived from a Center, a divine Center. Each one of us can live such a life of amazing power and peace and serenity, of integration and confidence and simplified multiplicity, on one condition—that is, *if we really want to.*[1]

There is a case to be made for the power of personal discipline and learned commitment. Randy writes,

> Scott believed in me long before I was ready to believe fully in myself. He was confident in my determination to finish Grandma's Mara-

thon in Duluth, Minnesota, long before I was ready for the race. He knew that for me to run a marathon for the first time would take motivation, perseverance and plain, old hard work. He should know, for his business is teaching physical wellness and training athletes for university-level competition. As he coached me, he became a mentor to me. He poured himself personally into my life as he instructed me, ran with me and then turned me loose for fifteen-to-eighteen-mile endurance tests. His accountability measures were timely, with a unique combination of a gentle hand of encouragement and a chiseling force of motivation. His exercises were the right amounts for the right time in my season of training.

What surprised me most about his coaching happened when I reached the peak of my conditioning a month before the race. Scott understood the dangers of overtraining for a marathon, especially as the day of the race approached. During my training I had never run farther than 18 miles, and I assumed that I was a long way from being able to complete the grueling long-distance race of 26.2 miles, but Scott wisely required a time of "down-training" to help me store up energy reserves for the race. Timely words spoken to my zealous impulses to run the full distance during my training continue to be a source of perspective when I think I need to "overtrain" in the race of life. He said, "You have trained well. You have built up your endurance through our training exercises that will carry you well beyond the 18-mile mark for the race. You need to trust me that this phase of your training is just as crucial as the previous one if you want to finish the race."

To finish a marathon race a runner needs commitment, perseverance, strength and stamina and is helped significantly by having someone to keep him or her accountable in training. Health demands exercise. We know that in our studies of physical wellness, but the principle holds for spiritual formation as well.

In this chapter we will provide practical questions, proposals for account-ability and examples of methods that can structure the mentoring relation-ship. We have waited until late in the book to provide such tools because we are persuaded that spiritual mentoring is not primarily a methodology but rather a relationship. It is not a list of steps, programs or "how tos" that a mentor will use as a recipe or formula. So we come to the questions of methods carefully, attentive to the need for first cultivating hospitality, trust, intimacy and friendship. The voices of Ignatius of Loyola and Jeanne Guyon urge us to develop spiritual health through exercise of our souls and provide measures of *accountability* in order for us to finish well the race of faith.

In order to create an effective relationship for mentoring, guides of the soul know that measures of *accountability* are necessary. Like the intense training that is accomplished through the accountability measures of the coach of a marathon runner, disciplined training through accountability measures is required to empower spiritual growth. No marathon runner would finish the race without the internal motivation that comes about through the training measures set up by the coach. Something happens to our motivation meter when someone issues a challenge wrapped with encouragement. So it goes with spiritual mentoring.

The mentor must insure that the mentoree is following through and getting the most out of the relationship, whether the assignments be implicit or explicit. The knowledge that he or she will be held accountable will stimulate a mentoree to make the most of the relational situation.[2]

The accountability dynamic describes the tangibles that will help to sustain and guide the relationship toward empowerment. What strength conditioning, cardiovascular conditioning and stamina development are to running, spiritual disciplines are to spiritual formation. They are not to be confused with the actual race as ends in themselves, but they are ways to prepare. They are not to be equated with the fullness of faith, though they create a mindset and a "heart-set" of attention and there is much of the faith in them. It is the task of the mentor to keep the mentoree accountable by assigning growth measures in timely progression. Since each mentoring relationship will have its own set of stories and dynamics, a one-size-fits-all regimen is not possible. Each situation requires its own accountability questions. Mentoring cannot be done from a simplistic fill-in-the-blank book that determines in advance the correct steps for all to follow in lock-step progression. Wisdom, discernment, adaptation, creative planning and thoughtful preparation are needed by the mentor.

Slow Growth
Spiritual formation is a slow process. Without the disciplines of spiritual

exercises, its pathway is random and chaotic. Spiritual disciplines move one slowly, even imperceptibly forward. Keith recalls recently sitting on a rock, enjoying a rare afternoon staring out at the waters of the Atlantic Ocean in South Florida.

> Far to the south a sailboat journeyed to the north, barely moving, or so it seemed. Closer to shore were speedboats, a large tanker and yachts motoring across the horizon. Noise and motion caught my attention, entertaining and preoccupying me—constant motion of the tides, waterfowl, other birds, people walking by deep in conversation. Suddenly I looked up to see the tiny form of the sailboat, barely visible now, nearly off the horizon. To my surprise the plodding, steady motion of wind and sail had moved the sailboat forward. A straight line of progress? No, more like a zigzag that followed puffs of wind and the motion of waves. Relentless forward progress? No, it seldom is in the wind, on the sea. More like tugging and pulling and weaving. When the wind is strong and sails are right, the speed can be breathtaking, and when the wind lags and the sails are slack, patient waiting is the order of the moment. On board there is always activity—hoisting sails, coming about, shifting directions, trimming the keel or waiting—but the sailor knows the discipline appropriate to the moment.

Spiritual disciplines are the exercises of learning to read the winds and discern the moment. The goal is to allow the wind into your sail. Spiritual exercises are intentional, regular practices that make growth possible. On the sailboat, the disciplines necessary to catch the wind are never seen as onerous tasks or empty rituals of work *unless* one dislikes sailing or forgets the purposes of life on board the boat. The rituals of getting a boat ready to sail are the equivalent of the spiritual disciplines we will describe throughout this chapter—they are the practices necessary for us to catch the wind of the Holy Spirit. We exercise such disciplines to make it possible for the winds to blow into the sails of our lives.

Spiritual accountability may be as simple as some basic questions offered by one spiritual director early in our work together:

☐ What were the highs and lows of your week?

☐ Were you faithful to follow the disciplines to which you committed yourself?

☐ What have you heard God saying to you in the experiences of your week?

Such questions invite reflection on the mentoree's own life. They take seriously what we have learned from nearly all of the spiritual writers of the past, that God's revelation is given in and to and through our own stories, experiences and senses. To fill our sails with the wind requires that we develop spiritual exercises appropriate to our lives. One of the greatest of those teachers of the past who showed us a clear pathway to accountability is Ignatius of Loyola.

Ignatius of Loyola (1491-1556)

Ignatius was born in 1491 in the castle of his wealthy Loyola family in the Basque country of Spain. He lived during one of the most significant periods of change in the history of the church. The fifteenth and sixteenth centuries saw dramatic shifts in political power, land distribution, education and ecclesiastical authority. During this time the church took on a new identity as a result of the Reformation.

> Ignatius lived in the era when feudalistic principalities were yielding place to the powerful central governments which were arising. Monarchs were growing strong by uniting separate provinces into nations, as Ferdinand (1452-1516) and Isabella (1474-1504) strove to do in Spain.... Overseas, Spain was enlarging her newly found empire and endeavoring to convert its natives to Christianity. . . . In northern Europe, religious unity was dissolving. Luther was excommunicated in 1521, the year of Ignatius' conversion at Loyola; and Henry VIII became head of the Anglican Church in 1531. Southern Europe was still one in faith; but there, as in the north, the people's ignorance of that faith and the consequent neglect of practice were often appalling. The Church was full of abuses and in need of reform "in head and members."[3]

Ignatius joined the army in 1517 and was wounded in the leg four years later in a battle on the French border. His injury proved to be a defining moment. He returned to recuperate in Loyola, where he was limited to sedentary activities that included reading a book called *The Life of Christ.* Through his reading he was converted to Christian faith and was moved to delve more deeply into other Christian writings, including *The Imitation of Christ* by Thomas à Kempis and numerous stories of Saint Francis.

His life had come to an intersection, and a choice was needed. He was tempted, on the one hand, by wealth, fame and power, but he was intrigued, on the other hand, by the simple spirituality of Saint Francis. In 1523 as he recuperated from his war wound, which left him partially crippled, Ignatius set out on a pilgrimage to Jerusalem. The story goes that he decided to sell all his worldly possessions and set off to the holy city dressed in sackcloth. His ship was detained for a long period in a port town called Manresa, where he lived for nearly a year. During this time he had an ecstatic, mystical experience that prompted him to begin a more serious study of the faith he had now chosen as his own. Through this experience he saw the vital importance of an educational foundation to significantly influence both church and society. During his own intellectual growth his convictions for educational reform grew firm.

As time passed, Ignatius "kept in the foreground of his thought the same basic outlook and goal he had conceived at Loyola and Manresa: to do everything for 'the service and praise of His Divine Majesty,' and to try 'to procure the praise, honor, and service of God our Lord'; the need to direct and order our life for 'the glory and praise of God.' "[4]

In the historical era of the Reformation Ignatius sought to bring about reform—a reform from within each individual. To Ignatius the life of the Christian was meant to be a dynamic force in society. Each Christian should be known for his or her "spiritual growth and energetic apostolic endeavor."[5] The prime motivation in the Christian life was to be found through the continued maintenance of one's intimate relationship with God. The heart of what Ignatius promoted through his reform from within can be seen in his classic work *Spiritual Exercises,* which was created to guide the believer in spiritual growth, maturity and service. Only thirty years later the conviction that motivated Ignatius became a reality of immense proportions. On his death in 1556, he had founded thirty-three colleges and had written what became a classic model of spiritual reform in his *Spiritual Exercises,* and he has continued throughout the centuries to have an impact on the spiritual thought and practice of the church.

Spiritual Exercises

The Spiritual Exercises was written as a manual for spiritual directors, but its directives present a timeless resource for spiritual mentors today. Its essence is to assist the mentor in guiding the mentoree toward spiritual maturity through prayer. Ignatius intended that his instructions would be used in a spiritual retreat setting of thirty days, yet the principles can be applied in various time frames.[6] In the context of the retreat the mentoree was directed through a process of "ridding the soul of all 'inordinate attachments,' the necessary preliminary to seeking and finding the will of God."[7] Such attachments of heart and soul keep one in slavery and hinder one from an ability to pay attention to the voice of God. Ignatius's definition of spiritual exercises offers a starting place for the practical work of spiritual mentoring.

> By the term "Spiritual Exercises" is meant every method of examination of conscience, of meditation, of contemplation, of vocal and mental prayer, and of other spiritual activities that will be mentioned later. For just as taking a walk, journeying on foot, and running are bodily exercises, so we call Spiritual Exercises every way of preparing and disposing the soul to rid itself of all inordinate attachments, and, after their removal, of seeking and finding the will of God in the disposition of our life for the salvation of our soul.[8]

We are formed spiritually through the ongoing mystery of the Holy Spirit as God brings to completion the good work begun in a believer's life. Paradoxically, there is nothing we can do to cause growth. Growth is a gift given as we learn to attend to the presence of God in our lives. The farmer in the field does not bring growth to seeds but stands before the mystery of growth, waiting. On the other hand, we can benefit from an understanding of the elements of nutrition, environment, sun, rain and the damage of weeds and marauding insects, and we can prepare the soil. Ignatian disciplines call us to the starting point, which is in prayer, and they evoke in us an Ignatian type of contemplation that involves a process of reading, meditation and prayer.

For Ignatius the mentor was one who understood that the primary active "voice" in the mentoring relationship belonged to God. Therefore, in order to discern what God wanted to accomplish in the life of the mentoree, the mentor needed to be familiar with contemplation and meditation, be seasoned in wise counsel, have a grasp of biblical and theological perspectives and, above all, have an authentic love for the mentoree. In the context of the relationship the mentor exercised patience, provided encouragement, articulated the process, shared wisdom for decision making, made the mentoree aware of the dynamic of spiritual warfare and discerned the overall receptivity level of the mentoree.

Spiritual mentoring had two primary purposes. First, Ignatius sought to foster the recognition of one's chosenness by God—a chosenness recognized through the intimacy of relationship with God. Second, *The Spiritual Exercises* is structured for the discernment of the will of God for one's unique service, as preparation for service.

To some people "spiritual discipline" is an oxymoron, for "spirit" represents freedom, anything but the regimented exercises of accountability. However, if we use the metaphor of "becoming free to sing," we are close to understanding. Freedom is given its wings by the composer who exercises numerous disciplines that give birth to harmony in composition. Chords are "heard" within the "laws" of musical composition. A song, by definition, is an arrangement of notes and chords into a purposeful, coherent composition. Freedom, by its very nature, is not an anarchy of chaotic randomness but depends on structures within the discipline of creativity. Spiritual discipline requires arrangement, attention to flow, awareness of harmonic rules and the exercise of accountability to laws of growth, formation and maturity. Without such discipline, growth remains limited, development haphazard and formation only partial. The goal is never to impose rigid exercises as ends in themselves. The goal is always maturity, "to equip the saints for the work of ministry, for building up the body of Christ, until all of us come to the unity of the faith and of the knowledge of the Son of God, to maturity, to the measure of the full stature of Christ. . . . We must grow up in every way into him who is the head, into Christ" (Eph 4:12-13, 15).

Guided Times of Reflection

One of the significant contributions from Ignatian disciplines is his instruction for guided times of reflection. Careful reflective thinking is a regular part of effective spiritual mentoring. We suggest there are four "looks" to the work of reflection:

☐ the look back
☐ the look through
☐ the look forward
☐ the look around

The *look back* uses *memory* to think back on the day, week, month or year recently completed in order to notice things we might have missed before. We are looking back with God in mind as we try to cooperate with God's intentions for our lives. How? Recall, remember and relive events, people and thoughts or feelings.

Find a quiet place where you can think carefully through significant events, conversations with people, thoughts and important feelings. Some people find it helpful to use a journal to write out their thoughts and memories of past experiences. Others use the journal to ponder their current thoughts and feelings. Use your memory as a kind of "instant replay" to look again at moments that seemed particularly rich in meaning for you.

Did particular thoughts cross your mind? Did you see any connections between this and other events or conversations of the day? Do you have any sense that God was speaking to you through the experiences of the day? Is any particular meaning forming for you in your reflection? Don't be in a hurry to interpret events. At this point, simply remember and relive them.

The *look through* uses *thinking* to see deeper meaning. To look through is to begin more carefully to see connections and meaning in the experiences of the recent past. What is "of God" in your recollection? Are there patterns of meaning that begin to emerge for you? What are the connections between the events, people and thoughts or feelings you have identified? Were there points of pain or suffering that stirred your compassion? Were there feelings of injustice that incite you to act? Is there a plot emerging for you, that is, a sense of coherence, direction or challenge for your life? Is there a persistent theme that appears for you in your thinking at this moment? Can you identify that theme with any particular idea, image or thought? (See appendix 4, "Developing a Personal Time Line.")

The *look forward* uses *imagination* to see future directions. What ideas, themes or decisions seem to be indicated as a result of your reflection? How might your life look different if you listen to the "still small voice" of persistent ideas, images or thoughts? Is there a direction God seems to be leading? Are there actions, thoughts or feelings that need to change for you? Does God seem to be calling you forward to something more, new or deeper? Is there a ministry focus that has started to become clearer for you? If you were to act on the promptings from your reflection, what would that look like in practical ways?

The *look around* uses *community* to see resources for shared ministry. Are there implications for your family, friends, church or community from the promptings identified thus far? What support will help you accomplish these new actions? Is there old business to finish with other people in order to move ahead? How might the community (of friends or church) become partners with you in any new kingdom enterprises? How might the community become partners with you in prayer, encouragement and emotional support? Do you have a desire to draw others into similar disciplines, ministries or ways of living? Who can help you be accountable for the new convictions, actions or ideas generated by your time of reflection? How will you share this with your mentor?

Ignatian Exercises

Better than almost anyone of his own time, Ignatius knew how to create "systems" of spiritual exercises to move people toward maturity. He divided *The Spiritual Exercises* into four weeks or groupings for the mentoree to journey through movements of prayer and focused contemplation under the direction of the spiritual director. Although he structured the retreat for thirty days, the concepts presented are helpful in providing an informal accountability structure for the mentoree. Simply put, the result of the *The Spiritual Exercises* is clarification and direction for a Spirit-led life. We propose that mentors see the description of "weeks" as helpful movements for spiritual attentiveness. Notice carefully the progression through which Ignatius took retreatants on their way to spiritual maturity. Apparently he saw each week as another step of training, another series of conditioning measures toward spiritual stamina and perseverance. We will describe his terms and then explain and give practical uses for them.

Preparation of the heart (first week). The mentoree focuses on purgation, or the purification of the soul from sin. To accomplish this he or she must surrender the intellect, will, imagination and emotions. In this phase the mentoree comes face to face with the facades in his or her life. Elsewhere we referred to this as clearing the debris from our lives. To purge the soul is to prepare the heart to listen. This can include a fearless inventory of one's life to see where barriers to faith exist or habits deter one from growth. It is an honest and sober assessment of one's own tendency toward sinfulness.

In the first phase, with the guidance of the mentor, the mentoree attempts to clear the way by purging heart, soul, habits and intentions. Ignatius seemed intent on "clearing the road" that the Messiah might be able to come in great power. He understood that we are capable of "quenching the spirit" through "inordinate attachments," that is, distractions, digressions, habits or sins that block our progress or keep us from knowing the will of God. Ignatius knew that many Christians drift spiritually. Thus this step of purgation or cleansing includes a daily examination of conscience in order to remove the impediments of sins and faults. Though this sort of self-examination is not a popular discipline today, a sober moral and spiritual inventory of the heart is essential to the spiritual journey. We stop and ponder our own persistence at disobedience. We stop and ponder distracting habits and debilitating deceptions. Ignatius saw that spiritual disciplines are helpful and necessary to rid the soul of attachments of heart and soul that prevent one from paying attention to the voice of God.

Virtues of the heart (second week). The mentoree seeks illumination through contemplation on the incarnation and virtues of Christ and on the invitation given by Christ to actively spread the kingdom. In this second phase the mentoree is helped to be more Christlike in thought and feeling. As a result, the mentoree responds to Christ's invitation to act in the world to bring about the kingdom. The mentoree's decisions regarding his or her life are influenced by contemplation of Christ's earthly ministry.

In the second phase the focus turns toward Christ. The Christ-centered focus of Ignatian spirituality guides us to contemplate the person and life of Jesus. To contemplate Christ as example, sovereign and true commander creates a sense of humility and helps to prompt Christlike choices as Ignatius directs.

> Let him desire and seek nothing except the greater praise and glory of God our Lord as the aim of all he does. For everyone must keep in mind that in all that concerns the spiritual life his progress will be in proportion to his surrender of self-love and of his own will and interests.[9]

Ignatius sought to take the retreatant ever deeper and further "to imitate and be in reality more like Christ our Lord."[10] To become like Christ requires an ever-increasing knowledge of God, which results in living as Christlike people, obedient to God's calling in our lives. One pastor said recently, "I have dozens of people in my church who desire to experience Christ but few who want to serve him, many who desire a tangible revelation from God but few willing to give themselves to rigorous study and knowledge of him."

Habits of the heart (third week). The mentoree seeks intimacy with God through contemplation of the sufferings of Christ. Included in this third phase is an invitation to the mentoree to associate his or her own personal sufferings with the sufferings of Christ, thereby taking on the character of Christ.

This third phase focuses our attention on the passion of Jesus in order that we might learn further to imitate our Lord. The suffering and death of Jesus open the way for our salvation and inspire our own lives of holiness.

> This is to consider that Christ suffers all this for my sins, and what I ought to do and suffer for him.[11]
>
> While one is eating, let him imagine he sees Christ our Lord and His disciples at table, and consider how He eats and drinks, how He looks, how He speaks, and then strive to imitate Him. In this way, his mind will be occupied principally with our Lord and less with the provision for the body. Thus he will come to greater harmony and order in the way he ought to conduct himself.[12]

The imitation of Christ calls to mind the writings of Thomas à Kempis and Brother Lawrence. Both suggested the discipline of increasing awareness of the mind of Christ. The mentoree can accomplish this through study, meditation on the suffering of Jesus and contemplation of the cost of discipleship.

Rewards of the heart (fourth week). In the final phase the mentoree seeks intimacy with God through the joys of Christ. Included in this phase is a celebration of the new life in Christ. In the celebration of God's redemption of sinners, the mentoree learns to pay attention to his or her own sense of destiny and purpose within God's salvation story.

The fourth phase focuses our attention on the love of God in order to help us attain the love of God. Meditation on the resurrection enables the joyful obedience of love. Ignatius comments:

> This is to consider all blessings and gifts as descending from above. Thus, my limited power comes from the supreme and infinite power

above, and so, too, justice, goodness, mercy, etc. descend from above as the rays of light descend from the sun, and as the waters flow from their fountains.[13]

He suggests a prayer that summarizes well his goal in all of these spiritual exercises.

Take, Lord, and receive all my liberty, my memory, my understanding and my entire will, all that I have and possess. Thou hast given all to me. To Thee, O Lord, I return it. All is Thine, dispose of it wholly according to Thy will. Give me Thy love and Thy grace, for this is sufficient for me.[14]

This regimen of spiritual exercises offers a practical paradigm for a mentor to use with a mentoree. Other names for the steps in Ignatius's paradigm are purgation, illumination, invitation and celebration. His steps provide a progression of discipline that begins with a hard look at ourselves and ends with several long gazes at Jesus. The first phase focuses on preparation of the heart. It is followed by attention to the virtues and habits of the life of Christ. The reward is knowing oneself as the beloved child of God and living the life of God's child in the world.

Practical Principles

Four major principles further guide the work of spiritual mentors in developing accountability with the mentoree: (1) adaptable hospitality, (2) intentionality and discipline, (3) imagination and (4) discernment.

1. *Adaptable hospitality.* Ignatius taught that a spiritual director should adapt the activities of spiritual guidance to the mentoree's age, ability, background and disposition. Forty chapters of instructions offer a wide variety of methods, questions, activities and ideas for the process. Throughout the process a spirit of sensitivity and adaptability should guide the work of the spiritual director.

When he who gives the Exercises finds that the exerciterant experiences no spiritual movements in his soul, such as consolations or desolations, nor is agitated by divers spirits, he ought to question him fully about the Exercises. . . . If he is found to be desolate or tempted, the director is to be kind and gentle, encouraging and strengthening him for the future, and it is suggested that the director should be faithfully informed of the various agitations and thoughts which the different spirits excite in him; because, according to the greater or less profit he finds, his director may be able to give him some suitable spiritual exercises adapted to the needs of a soul thus agitated.[15]

John of the Cross would heartily agree with Ignatius. John said,

God leads each one along different paths so that hardly one spirit will be found like another in even half its method or procedure.[16]

A story by way of illustration may help. Randy was looking forward to the midwinter faculty retreat, as were his colleagues from the seminary.

Something about being still at the Benedictine Blue Cloud Abbey in the vastness of the South Dakota prairie brings about a quiet purpose, perspective and peace in its own peculiar way. Sister Del Rey was our host for the retreat, a gentle, yet spiritually strong woman known for her ability to help you "listen to your life." Being trained in the Ignatian *Spiritual Exercises*, Sister Del Rey understood what it meant to "listen to the moment" in the movement of prayer and the movement of life in a community.

After group prayers we returned to our rooms for individual reflection on several prescribed scriptural passages. We were also invited to visit with Sister Del Rey individually if we wished. It offered an opportunity simply to be listened to or to pray together. I waited in my room for a while, knowing, however, that I would eventually meander down the hall and meet with this woman whose spirit created an attraction of curiosity. I entered her study with anticipation and a readiness for spiritual exploration. Her procedure was simple: she asked me why I came and invited me to tell her the story of my journey in faith. As I described my story to this seasoned woman of discernment, strength and compassion, I knew I was in the presence of one who knew God. Her attentiveness to my story, which was expressed through her discerning eyes, created a mixture of feelings. Although I longed for that intense consideration, her eyes made me uneasy. Someone was actually hosting me, welcoming me and listening with compassionate attention. I felt as if she knew a great deal about me though we had just met a few short hours earlier.

I remember the times when, growing up as a little boy in the Catholic church in Yorkton, Saskatechewan, I was blessed by Father Mike. Although I am still not sure of the exact words he said to me, I remember them as words of significance. As Father Mike held my head between his two large hands, he would look into my eyes and bless me with a prayer that always left me with a sense of acceptance and purpose.

As my time with Sister Del Rey drew to a close, I knew without a doubt the final question I wanted to ask. I told her of Father Mike and his way of blessing me as a child. Feeling too embarrassed now simply to ask her to bless me, I cleverly rewrapped my question in the language of ministry, an inquiry from one ministry professional to another. "So, Sister Del Rey, what do you think about the notion of blessing people through your ministry?"

Immediately her face broke into a warm smile. She gave me the look of indulging a child and said to me, "Randy, would you mind if I put my hand on your forehead?" Without many words or elaborate ceremony, she placed her arthritic hands on my head and blessed me. I felt renewed once again in my acceptance and purpose.

For Reflection

☐ What keeps you from believing your life can be a blessing?
☐ Where do you long for a blessing in your life?
☐ Who needs a blessing from your hands?
☐ Who has given you a blessing for your life? Recently? In the past?

Learning Discernment

The collection of spiritual exercises for spiritual direction is not a cookbook with simple recipes to be followed woodenly and literally. Discernment of methods, what we call adaptable hospitality, is an essential function of the spiritual director. Kenneth Leech says, "*The Spiritual Exercises* are a treasury of spirituality, and the purpose of them is to enable the individual, with good direction, to discover the right form of prayer for him. 'Our Father wanted us, in all our activities, as far as possible to be free, at ease in ourselves, and obedient to the light given particularly to each one.' 'The Father said to me that there can be no greater mistake in his view of the spirit than to want to mold others in one's own image.' "[17]

Ignatius classified the discernment of the Spirit into two categories, which he called consolations and desolations.

> I call it consolation when an interior movement is aroused in the soul, by which it is inflamed with love of its Creator and Lord.... It is likewise consolation when one sheds tears that move to the love of God, whether it be because of sorrow or sins or because of the suffering of Christ our Lord.... Finally, I call consolation every increase of faith, hope, and love, and all interior joy that invites and attracts to what is heavenly and to the salvation of one's soul by filling it with peace and quiet in its Creator and Lord.[18]

> I call desolation what is entirely the opposite of what is described in the third rule, as darkness of soul, turmoil of spirit, inclination to what is low and earthly, restlessness rising from many disturbances and temptations which lead to want of faith, want of hope, want of love.[19]

The amazing practicality of his rules for discernment are illustrated by three of his warnings to those in the midst of desolation.

> In time of desolation we should never make any change but remain firm and constant in the resolution and decision which guided us the day before the desolation.

> When one is in desolation, he should be mindful that God has left him to his natural powers to resist the different agitations and temptations of the enemy in order to try him.

> When one is in desolation, he should strive to persevere in patience.[20]

2. *Intentionality and discipline.* Some see the Ignatian exercises as strict, stern or rigid. We see them instead as intensive and intentional. Ignatius brought together, as we do in this chapter, a variety of practices, exercises and suggestions for retreatants as a model for mentoring practices. The principle of adaptability suggests that methods need to be personalized to the life and needs of the mentoree as discerned by the mentor. Ignatius also perceived that the spiritual guide ought to remain secondary, in the background, so that

God's work can be accomplished. The mentor needs to trust the existing action of God in the life of the mentoree.

> The director of the Exercises, as a balance at equilibrium, without leaning to one side or the other, should permit the Creator to deal directly with the creature, and the creature directly with his Creator and Lord.[21]

As Leech comments, "He gives instructions about place of prayer, environment, control of the body and the mind, mental recollection, composition and use of imagination, preparatory prayers and so on."[22]

A six-part model is given near the end of *The Spiritual Exercises*. It is a pattern to be followed by the spiritual director in mentoring the retreatant. The spiritual director was instructed to

☐ urge the practice of regular daily meditation

☐ conduct a daily examination of conscience in which the mentorees will carefully study the events of the day to see where they have strayed from God's intentions for their lives

☐ lead the mentorees to weekly confession and communion

☐ suggest that "he should choose some good confessor and take him for his guide in this spiritual journey, treating with him of everything that concerns his soul"

☐ lead the mentoree to the practice of spiritual reading fellowship with other Christians

☐ urge daily growth in virtues.[23]

3. *Imagination.* Through careful processes of reading the Scripture, meditative thought and prayer, one is able to contemplate more fully the person and character of God. The goal of such contemplation is that one will be consoled.

> I will call back into my memory the gifts I have received—my creation, redemption, and other gifts particular to myself. I will ponder with deep affection how much God our Lord has done for me, and how much he has given me of what he possesses, and consequently how he, the same Lord, desires to give me even his very self, in accordance with his divine design.
>
> Then I will reflect on myself, and consider what I on my own part ought in all reason and justice to offer and give to his Divine Majesty, namely, all my possessions, and myself along with them. I will speak as

one making an offering with deep affection and say:

Take, Lord, and receive all my liberty, my memory, my understanding, and all my will—all that I have and possess. You, Lord, have given all that to me. I now give it back to you, O Lord. All of it is yours. Dispose of it according to your will. Give me your love and your grace, for that is enough for me.[24]

Ignatius had a wonderful insight into the value of imagination in the life of the Spirit. Sometimes considered a bad thing in Christian circles, imagination or image-making is a faithful act of the heart to see with spiritual eyes what God is doing. Jesus' oft-repeated words are a call to imagine what is not yet fully present, the kingdom of God: "He who has ears, let him hear" (Mt 11:15 NIV). With ears to hear and eyes to see, we exercise the faith of seeing the world as God sees it; perhaps the clearest statement of our goal is to see as God sees and to love as God loves.

Practical guidance is the signature of Ignatian spiritual direction, but so is a wonderfully inspired use of the imagination. He instructs retreatants to call to mind people, situations, memories and thoughts. One of his instructions is, for example, "The Fifth contemplation: This will consist in applying the five senses to the matter of the first and second contemplations."[25] Long before guided-imagery meditation was a popular or widely used method of contemplation, Ignatius was guiding people to use their minds, imaginations and senses to enhance their spiritual growth. He wrote, "When the contemplation or meditation is on something visible, for example, when we contemplate Christ our Lord, the representation will consist in seeing in imagination the material place where the object is we wish to contemplate. I said the material place, for example, the temple or the mountain where Jesus or His Mother is."[26]

I will call to mind all the sins of my life, reviewing year by year and period by period.[27]

I will consider who I am, and by means of examples humble myself:
1. Who am I compared with all men?
2. What are all men compared with the angels and saints of paradise?
3. Consider what all creation is in comparison with God. Then I alone, what can I be?[28]

4. *Discernment.* Ignatius provided a practical methodology for the work of

diakrisis or discernment of the spirit. Prior to Ignatius the focus of discernment was on attitudes, virtues and one's state of life; he moved the focus to actions in concrete situations of life. Ignatius offered practical and useful disciplines for decision making and discernment with questions like these: If you were at the moment of death, what would you choose to do? If you were to picture an unknown person you would like to see practice perfection, what should this person decide to do in this particular situation?

For Ignatius a purpose of the spiritual disciplines was to learn to see God in all things. One very practical exercise for his retreatants was to look back over the day and attempt to see it as God saw it. In our quest for leadership skills and strategy we have neglected perhaps the more critical issue, the formation of character through recognizing God's sovereign shaping of our stories, even before we recognized we were being shaped (Ps 139:13-16). In *The Healing Power of Stories* Daniel Taylor talks about the "story quality of our own lives":

> Seeing our lives as stories, rather than as an unrelated series of random events, increases the possibility for having in our lives what we find in the best stories: significant, purposeful action. We all want very much for it to have mattered that we were here. If nothing in the universe is different, even better, because I exist, then I am hard pressed to justify my next breath. It is difficult for me to see why anything I am or do is meaningful unless I begin to understand my connectedness to others, to the past, and to the future. That connectedness is primarily the connectedness of story—of lives interwoven over time in a purposeful plot. Understanding my life in this way gives me better reasons than I otherwise have to live life with optimism and courage.[29]

In the shared work of mentoring we learn how to see connections, how to recognize plot and how to enjoy the unfolding story line of our own lives and the lives of others, but it takes the discipline of noticing, the practice of attention, to make those connections. It requires the art of asking good questions, something that can be developed. It takes the courage to hold another accountable to implicit and explicit tasks for formation.

Ignatius was especially insistent, as we are, that we learn to see God in all things, to notice the presence of God in every place, to hear, see, smell, touch and taste with a new awareness, a new carefulness and a deepened alertness.

In the earliest years of church life, theology (talking *about* God) was not separated from spirituality (which included talking *to* God). The early church father Anselm spoke of "faith seeking theology," by which he meant that doctrine and prayer belong together, just as reflective thinking about the actual events of life is essential to making meaning in our lives. Ignatian methods may be difficult for many in our frantically busy world, but reflective living is surely not impossible for any of us. Even as we wait at the traffic light, can we not lift a prayer? As we wait in line at the bank, can we not think about the moments of our day? As we drive everywhere, can we turn off the radio, tapes and CDs and listen reflectively to the events of our day? Certainly the discipline of creating time for reflection is a lifeline for spiritual health. Without times in quiet, thoughtful reflection, our spirituality remains shallow, anemic and misguided.

In the Ignatian exercises there was an "examen of conscience" at the end of the day, a time to reflect on all that you had done wrong since last you were in that place.

> He should demand an account of himself with regard to the particular point which he was resolved to watch in order to correct himself and improve. Let him go over the single hours or periods of time from the time he arose to the hour and moment of the present examination, and . . . make a mark for each time that he has fallen into the particular sin or defect. Then he is to renew his resolution, and strive to amend during the time till the second examination is to be made.[30]

Some suggest today as well an "examen of consciousness" that thanks God for the gift of the day and seeks to discern how God's Spirit was moving throughout the day, in conscience *and* in consciousness. It is a review of the day with God through conversation. It is the spiritual discipline of telling your own story and seeing in it the importance of plots, subplots, themes and the development of character. Spiritual formation requires an intention to live the examined life, the reflective life, a life that alertly seeks the presence of God in everything. In the holy relationship of spiritual mentoring, both the mentor and the mentoree are to "take the raw material newly objectified, and interpret its meaning in terms of God's calling, challenging, leading, etc. This material constitutes a type of 'life-hermeneutic.' "[31]

Suggested questions for accountability include the following:

☐ What were the events of my day, that is, what happened as I lived the past day of my life?

☐ Were there any whispers from God or hints of God's presence in the events of this day?

☐ What questions do I have that I might want to ask God as I conclude this day?

☐ What disappointments did I have during this day? Are they irreparable? Redeemable?

☐ In what ways am I aware of living within God's will through this day?

☐ In what ways am I aware of living outside of God's will through this day?

☐ Are there words of confrontation that God might wish to speak to me?

☐ Are there words of consolation that God might wish to speak to me?

☐ Are there words of encouragement and challenge that God might wish to speak to me?

☐ Whom did I encounter today?

☐ Where was I anxious and afraid today?

The Discipline of Questions

Just as effective teaching engages the learner in multiple learning activities, so spiritual mentoring will creatively make use of three categories or types of questions. Thomas Groome calls these questions of critical reason, analytical memory and creative imagination.

Critical reason questions take such forms as

☐ What do we think this means and why?

☐ What is life-giving here and why?

☐ What is not life-giving here and why not?

☐ Whose interest is being served?

☐ Who is suffering?

☐ What are some of the reasons for this present state of affairs?

☐ Can you explain some of your own attitudes?

Analytical memory is encouraged by such questions as

☐ How did this present situation arise?

☐ What is the history—personal or social—behind it?

☐ Whose interests brought things to be this way?

☐ What memories does this hold for you?
☐ What are some of the roots of your own attitude?
☐ Can you share some of the story behind what you're saying (or feeling, or doing)?

Creative imagination is encouraged by such questions as
☐ What are the likely consequences of this?
☐ What should be the outcome here?
☐ What can we do on behalf of what is best for all?
☐ What changes can we make that are fitting?
☐ What consequences would we prefer and how do we help to shape them?
☐ How do you feel called to respond?
☐ What would I mean to act *for life for all*?[32]

The underlying purpose of all three types of questions is the same: to move the mentoree to pay attention to the presence (and Voice) of God in everything. This is the ultimate purpose—to see or hear in such a way that I heed. The mentor brings no preconceived template of answers, blueprint of spiritual architecture or even preferred personal outcomes. Spiritual mentoring is not about what the mentor wants or even about what the mentoree wants. It is ever and always about attention to the still small voice of God. Thus it becomes one of the hardest ministries for people today because we often tend to believe we know what is best for another's life.

The questions are important for several purposes:
☐ to engage you in thoughtful reflection about your own experience of spirituality
☐ to invite you to think more deeply, more sacramentally, about what otherwise might appear to be merely daily events
☐ to incite you to love and good works for the sake of others as a result of your spiritual reflection, and thus to transform our world

In her little book *Learning to Listen: A Guide for Spiritual Friends*, Wendy Miller has a provocative list of questions that could be helpful for the mentor and the mentoree.

What is my prayer experience like?
What happens when I pray or meditate on Scripture?
What areas of my life is God touching?
How am I experiencing God's grace?

What is God like for me—in Scripture, in times of prayer or other times?
How have I cooperated with God this week (month)?
What am I not bringing openly before God (for example, anger or fear)?
Where have I missed experiencing God's grace or love?
What do I need to confess?
What is changing within me as I listen to God?
What attitudes am I experiencing as I relate to others in my life?[33]

Lectio Divina

Another classical discipline of spiritual formation is *lectio divina*, "sacred reading." Much of what passes for spiritual direction in the church today is more like junk food than a nourishing meal. Often Bible study consists of a brief half-page devotional, the predigested thoughts of others or the pooled ignorance of feelings-dominated Bible studies in which the primary question is "What does this passage mean to you?" Biblical illiteracy is increasing at a terrifying pace. Even those who know the content of the Bible often lack understanding. *Lectio divina* is a means of contemplating on the Word of God as we read it slowly and linger over its meaning just as we might linger over a nourishing dinner with friends.

Sacred reading requires time, regularity and care. This is an unchanging axiom in the life of the Spirit. We need to read the Scriptures consistently and often. If we are unfamiliar with the Bible's words, we have a spirituality based on other human voices rather than on God's voice. We are deaf to God's voice if we refuse to listen and refuse to open the book that reveals God's voice. Do we believe any more that the word of God is quick and powerful, sharper than any two-edged sword? Do we believe it is the word of life that can transform, renew and create? Does our practice reflect our spoken beliefs?

Reflection on the Bible is indispensable to one's spiritual growth. Could it be that a fourteenth-century woman such as Julian of Norwich living in the isolation of a monastic community might become the voice that calls us back to the sacred reading and sacred hearing and sacred heeding of God's word spoken in Holy Scripture? She wrote,

> God showed me the very great delight that he has in all men and women who accept, firmly and humbly and reverently, the preaching and teaching of Holy Church, for he is Holy Church. For he is the

foundation, he is the substance, he is the teaching, he is the teacher, he is the end, he is the reward for which every faithful soul labors; and he is known and will be known to every soul to whom the Holy Spirit declares this. And I am certain that all who seek in this way will prosper, for they are seeking God.[34]

Lectio divina will always draw us back to the three questions that we have identified as indispensable to our spiritual growth: Who is God? Who am I? What am I to do with my life? These three remind us of our need for intimacy with God, identity as the beloved of God and agency for kingdom responsibility. First, sacred reading will help us to understand the character of the God of Abraham and Sarah, Isaac and Rebekah, Jacob and Rachel. It will lead us to see God as motivated by an endless desire to know us intimately. Second, sacred reading will help us understand ourselves as the beloved daughters and sons of God. We distort that reading when we see ourselves as those despised or rejected by the God of love. God's wrath is a necessary part of God's love, but even in that wrath we hear the truth: "While we still were sinners Christ died for us" (Rom 5:8). Finally, sacred reading will propel us outward into the world with empowered voices to speak gospel from our own unique and creative word to the world.

Augustine, writing in his *Confessions*, tells of the importance of God's Word for his life. While reading a passage in Paul's letter to the Romans, Augustine was overwhelmed by his encounter with its truth and with God in the Word. Though he devoted much of his life to philosophy, Scripture remained a pivotal part of his study. Through Scripture, Jesus became the object of his deep affection and love.

The church today has a deep need for this kind of biblical knowledge and understanding. Biblical ignorance spreads dysfunction to every part of ecclesial life—unbiblical thinking, unbiblical behavior, unbiblical worship and unbiblical leadership principles. Most damaging, however, is an ever-increasing loss of intimacy with the One whom God called *Logos*, "the Word," Jesus Christ. It is clear that many have not learned how to study the sacred book.

Four Disciplines in the Curriculum of Christlikeness

Dallas Willard has summarized well four practices we believe can be suggested helpfully by the mentor at appropriate moments in the life of the mentoree. Willard believes the following four disciplines are foundational for growth as apprentices of Jesus:

Two disciplines of abstinence: solitude and silence.
Two disciplines of positive engagement: study and worship.[35]

Solitude is understood by Willard as a lengthy time of being out of contact with people, while silence means "to escape from sounds, noises, other than the gentle ones of nature. . . . Both dimensions of silence are critical for the breaking of old habits and the formation of Christ's character in us. . . . They break the pell-mell rush through life and create a kind of inner space that permits people to become aware of what they are doing and what they are *about* to do."[36]

It has been the almost unison voice of spiritual teachers throughout history that people need regular periods of time when they choose to be quiet. The sabbath teachings of the Old Testament show us that God intended a weekly time for us to stop, cease and desist, for that is the literal meaning of the word *sabbath*. On the seventh day of creation, God worked. The misconception is that God did nothing, but it is more accurate to say that God's work on the seventh day, the sabbath, was the work of rest.

It is in *study*, says Willard, "that we place our minds fully upon God and his kingdom. And study is brought to its natural completion in the worship of God."[37] In order for the mentoree to become a true follower of Jesus, he or she must understand what Jesus did and what he calls his followers to do. Study requires a concentrated attention on Jesus, on the written words of Scripture and on others who have learned to be followers of Jesus. Paul outlined the discipline of study in Philippians 4:8-9:

Finally, beloved, whatever is true, whatever is honorable, whatever is just, whatever is pure, whatever is pleasing, whatever is commendable, if there is any excellence and if there is anything worthy of praise, *think about these things*. Keep on doing the things that you have learned and received and heard and seen in me, and the God of peace will be with you.

There is no room for ignorance in the lives of kingdom people. Jesus is first brought to us as *teacher*. As *disciples* (the root word of *discipline*), we are *learners.*

> Worship ... imprints on our whole being the reality that we study. The effect is a radical disruption of the powers of evil in us and around us. Often an enduring and substantial change is brought about. And the renewal of worship keeps the glow and power of our true homeland an active agent in all parts of our being. To "hear and do" in the atmosphere of worship is the clearest, most obvious and natural thing imaginable.[38]

In his thorough and profound book *The Divine Conspiracy*, Willard articulates a case for these four—solitude and silence, study and worship—as essential disciplines in the curriculum for Christlikeness.

Experiencing Christ Through Scripture and Prayer

Jeanne Guyon (1648-1717) was born in France and has become recognized as one of the most influential Christian writers in the history of the church. Her acclaimed book *Experiencing the Depths of Jesus Christ* has been called one of the most influential books ever to be written in the history of the church. It is compelling in its simplicity and clarity. It is wide-reaching in its scope. Few books on spiritual life and prayer speak with such innocent power and have such an amazing ability to motivate spiritual discipline. Movements such as the Quakers, Zinzendorf and the Moravians and religious leaders such as John Wesley and Watchman Nee are among those who have been shaped by her thoughts and perspectives. Her work has "influenced the lives of more famous Christians than perhaps any other piece of Literature penned in the last 300 years."[39]

Jeanne Guyon proclaimed a prophetic message of the need for a return to intimacy with God at a time when the church was being heavily influenced by political and ecclesiastical power structures. Because the people understood correct doctrine, they assumed that had attained correct standing before God. As Edwards boldly comments, in the church in Guyon's day as in the present day, the church leadership is often "enamored with the gifts, yet hardly knowing the Giver."[40] Guyon's prophetic word was a cry to the church to return to relationship with the Giver, a conversion that she believed would bring significant social and political transformation. Prayer will change society! Prayer will bring healing! Prayer will restore the church to health!

Madame Guyon taught that there are two ways to come to intimacy with

the Lord. These she called "praying the Scripture" and "beholding the Lord."
There are few techniques or spiritual exercises more desperately needed today
than learning the discipline of "praying the Scripture." Her own words speak
most simply:

> Here is how you should begin.
>
> Turn to the Scripture; choose some passage that is simple and fairly
> practical. Next, come to the Lord. Come quietly and humbly. There,
> before Him, read a small portion of the passage of Scripture you have
> opened to.
>
> Be careful as you read. Take in fully, gently and carefully what you
> are reading. Taste it and digest it as you read.
>
> In the past it may have been your habit, while reading, to move very
> quickly from one verse of Scripture to another until you had read the
> whole passage. Perhaps you were seeking to find the main point of the
> passage.
>
> But in coming to the Lord by means of "praying the Scripture," you
> do not read quickly; you read very slowly. You do not move from one
> passage to another, not until you have sensed the very heart of what you
> have read.
>
> You may then want to take that portion of Scripture that has touched
> you and turn it into prayer.[41]

"Beholding the Lord" for Jeanne Guyon meant a time for "waiting on the
Lord."

> The way to do this is really quite simple.
>
> First, read a passage of Scripture. Once you sense the Lord's pres-
> ence, the content of what you have read is no longer important. The
> Scripture has served its purpose; it has quieted your mind; it has brought
> you to Him.
>
> You begin by setting aside a time to be with the Lord. When you
> do come to Him, come quietly. Turn your heart to the presence of God.
> How is this done? This, too, is quite simple. You turn to Him by faith.
> By faith you believe you have come into the presence of God.
>
> Next, while you are before the Lord, begin to read the same portion
> of Scripture.

As you read, pause.

The pause should be quite gentle. You have paused so that you may set your mind on the Spirit. You have set your mind inwardly—on Christ.[42]

Further Reflection for the Mentor

1. What basic "start-up" questions, methods or disciplines can you draw from the work of Ignatius and Jeanne Guyon?

2. How might you proceed to take a person deeper in their imitation of Christ?

3. Have you experienced any of these spiritual disciplines in your own life? Which one(s) have been the most help to you personally? Why?

Further Reflection for the Mentoree

James Fowler offers several additional questions that can help us notice reality.

What are you spending and being spent for?

What commands and receives your best time and energy?

What goals, dreams or institutions are you pouring out your life for?

As you live your life, what power or powers do you fear or dread?

What powers do you rely on and trust?

With whom or with what group do you share your most sacred or private hopes for your life and for the lives of those whom you love?

What are those most sacred and compelling hopes and purposes in your life?[43]

Seven

The Goal of Spiritual Mentoring
Empowerment

It is extremely rare to find a person who rejoices in his own uniqueness,
who enjoys that bit of God's handiwork which is herself.[1]

GORDON COSBY

One of the most compelling stories of someone discovering her voice is that of a woman who became deaf and blind at the age of nineteen months; her name is Helen Keller. Her teacher was Anne Mansfield Sullivan, a graduate of the Perkins Institution for the Blind in Boston, a woman who refused to believe the popular wisdom of the day that someone like Helen could not be educated. Anne set out to teach Helen everything she could. Anne taught her Braille so Helen could learn to read and write. She taught Helen to speak by having Helen listen with her fingers. She would press Helen's fingers on her own larynx so Helen could hear vibrations, and she eventually helped Helen to rediscover her own voice.

The process of spiritual mentoring couldn't be better described than in this moving story of a relationship that led to empowerment and voice for one whom most saw as unable to speak, ineducable and, therefore, unworthy. As mentor, Anne helped Helen Keller by creating a relationship of trust and taking the time necessary for Helen's own voice to be freed to give expression to all that lay within her. As mentoree, Helen brought a teachable spirit, a hungry and capable mind, curiosity and readiness to learn all that she could. Together, they created disciplines for teaching and learning, inventing curriculum and pedagogy as they went. The results were stunning: Helen rediscovered her voice!

In this chapter we will concentrate on the effect in spiritual mentoring of paying attention to the already present action of God. We refer to this as the discovery of one's unique voice. To speak in terms of goals within the context of spiritual mentoring presents an inherent danger of planning for measurable results. In fact, to speak of goals or empowerment may sound contradictory to our discussion thus far. However, it is imperative for the responsible mentor to consider the question "How will I know if my mentoree has been mentored spiritually?" Perhaps the obvious answer is a changed life—to be more specific, a changed life that has come to understand the relationship between ultimate identity and ultimate purpose. Freeing the soul to sing is that process by which intimacy with God and understanding one's ultimate identity as the beloved of God allow for expression of one's unique voice in concrete and practical works of the reign of God among us.

We are convinced that God has placed within each person a unique voice for ministry. Through mentoring we are helped to listen to God's song so that we may give voice to that song in a way that is unique to each of us. As we listen to the music that sings in the heart of God, the music inside us is given voice. Our voices will sing with words, tone, accent, timber and pitch that are ours alone. Our voices will sing from a history, posture and perspective that is ours alone. As people created in the image of the God, who created by giving voice to his commands, we reflect that image or perhaps echo that voice through the personal expression of our own voices. We believe the image of voice is more than mere metaphor; it is an empowered way to release that which God has implanted in all people. Annie Dillard said, "You were made and set here for this, to give voice to your own amazement."[2]

A healthy mentoring relationship should help you to give voice to the song God has sung into your life, to liberate the song that has lain dormant or imprisoned in your history. You should be able to sing the song with your own voice, in your own way, as a response of joy to the amazement of hearing God sing to you. Through spiritual mentoring you will freely and vigorously exercise your God-given gifts in a ministry that is equally God-given. You will discover the voice within and let it ring out!

The letters of Paul speak of the sovereign democracy of spiritual giftedness.

To each is given the manifestation of the Spirit for the common good.
(1 Cor 12:7)
But each of us was given grace according to the measure of Christ's
gift. (Eph 4:7)

Yours may be a song of joy, but it could just as well be a song of lament. It
may be a song of peace, but it could just as easily be a song of prophetic
challenge to systems enslaved in evil. Your voice will reflect the holy history
of your own life and its experiences.

The church has forgotten at times that faith is narrated in the holy, sacred
experiences of individual lives. Jesus incarnated God's song in the holy history
of his life as a politically oppressed, economically marginalized, socially
segregated Semite living in rural Palestine in the first century. His song rang
with the accents of his Jewish culture. His song rang with the tones of his
experiences in rural Galilee and the small cities of northern Israel. When he
gave voice to the story God placed in him, not all welcomed its message, not
all believed his storied truth, and some moved ultimately to silence it by
crucifixion and death.

Our voices may tell stories that run counter to a culture that prefers the
banal jingles manufactured to maneuver us ever more noisily to the malls of
our land. For too long the voice of the church has been a strong echo of these
banalities rather than a strong echo of the voice of our Creator. Psalm 12:1-2
cries out,

Help, O LORD, for there is no longer anyone who is godly;
the faithful have disappeared from humankind.
They utter lies to each other;
with flattering lips and a double heart they speak.

Healthy children do not need to be taught to give voice to that which is
within; they naturally respond with curious amazement to the new world in
which they find themselves. It is an unfortunate conspiracy of adults and
painful experiences that stifles a child. Psalm 38:12-14 comments,

Those who seek my life lay their snares;
those who seek to hurt me speak of ruin,
and meditate treachery all day long.
But I am like the deaf, I do not hear;

like the mute, who cannot speak.
Truly, I am like one who does not hear,
 and in whose mouth is no retort.

The psalmist would prefer that we give voice to our own amazement.

I will sing of your steadfast love, O LORD, forever;
 with my mouth I will proclaim your faithfulness to all generations.
I declare that your steadfast love is established forever;
 your faithfulness is as firm as the heavens. (Ps 89:1-2)

It is good to give thanks to the LORD,
 to sing praises to your name, O Most High;
to declare your steadfast love in the morning,
 and your faithfulness by night,
to the music of the lute and the harp,
 to the melody of the lyre.
For you, O LORD, have made me glad by your work;
 at the works of your hands I sing for joy. (Ps 92:1-4)

O sing to the LORD a new song;
 sing to the LORD, all the earth.
Sing to the LORD, bless his name;
 tell of his salvation from day to day.
Declare his glory among the nations,
 his marvelous works among all the peoples. (Ps 96:1-3)

An ordinary life is rich with its own musical notes, rhythms and themes. There are sweet harmonies when the sounds make sense and evoke joy; there are harsh cacophonies of dissonance and disharmony when the music of life clashes with our souls. There are also moments of deafness when we hear none of the notes of our own music and wonder if we ever will again. Anyone can make music as all children do, spontaneously, freely and imaginatively, but discipline is required if we are to compose as adults the grand symphony of the soul.

God has already placed within you a song that is waiting to be released. As music lovers anticipate the release of a popular artist's new song, so your life longs for the release of the song of your soul. A spiritual mentor can help you hear the music that is being composed within, empowering you to hear and discern its themes until finally your own voice rings with the song. Eugene Peterson echoes the notion of our unique voice:

> Something very different takes place in the life of faith: each person discovers all the elements of a unique and original adventure. We are prevented from following in another's footsteps and are called to an incomparable association with Christ. The Bible makes it clear that every time that there is a story of faith, it is completely original. God's creative genius is endless. He, never fatigued and unable to maintain the rigors of creativity, never resorts to mass-producing copies. Each life is a fresh canvas on which he uses lines and colors, shades of lights, textures and proportions that he has never used before.[3]

A Window to the World

Many of the classical writers would be excellent choices for teaching the soul to sing. Our first choice is a spiritual mentor from England, Julian of Norwich.

Not much is known of Julian's early life except that she was an anchoress living in her monastic cell at the church of Saint Julian and Saint Edward at Carrow. As an anchoress she was restricted to her cell, where she would spend most days alone in prayer and work. One of her significant contributions to Christendom was her understanding of the immensity of the love of God. As a young woman, she prayed that God would give her a deeper, more profound sense of the passion of Jesus. It wasn't until she was thirty years old that she had her prayer answered. She lay deathly ill when she was confronted with a vision of Jesus, who spoke with her over the period of a day and a half. She dates the revelations May 13, 1373, in the presence of her mother and her parish priest. Her writings describe the visions she received.

Julian's life, at a time known for the black plague, the ravaging effects of the Hundred Years War and the Great Papal Schism, was a model for others to follow. During this dark time in history, her faith was one many desired to emulate. Margery Kempe, the English mystic, had frequent visits with Julian for spiritual mentoring. Her writings provide the meager biographical information we have regarding Julian.

The anchorholds were cells connected to a church sanctuary. The architecture of Julian's cell offers metaphoric insight into the dynamic of the empowerment of voice. The cells were situated around the sanctuary, each containing two windows. One window faced inward to the sanctuary; the other faced outward in the direction of the world outside the church.

The metaphorical implications of this physical setting are many. Julian, while committed to the development of the inner life in her anchorhold, was open to the outer world for the sake of the gospel. As she concentrated and committed her life to the development of her own soul, she kept her window open to the world. It is a wonderful picture of the inner life of prayer, meditation and devotion placed alongside the outer world of teaching, serving and loving others. Within her cell she kept her inner window open to interior life of worship and prayer. Through the outer window she developed a ministry of spiritual guidance and discernment for those who sought her out for her pastoral wisdom, for which she was renowned in the fourteenth century.

We need always to ponder the inner journey as it influences the outer journey of our spirituality and to consider how the outer journey, in fact, shapes the practices of the inner journey. We need always to ask about our own windows of ministry to the larger world. How are we nourished, equipped and empowered by the inner life of prayer, meditation and devotion, and what windows has God opened for ministry and service to others? If we live in cells with walls and no windows to the rest of the world, how faithful can we be to a God who loves us in order to give expression to our voice in society?

In 1373 Julian was near death when a priest was called in to administer her last rites. The priest had asked her to concentrate on the crucifix he held before her and to focus particularly on the face of her Lord. At that moment she received her sixteen showings or revelations of God's intimate love.

Some years before the incident she had asked God to give her in her thirtieth year an illness "which might seem, to her and to all others, as if it would be mortal, and for the gift of three wounds, of true contrition, loving compassion and longing with her will for God."[4] She hoped for an understanding of Christ's passion through some serious bodily sickness by which her faith could be tried and strengthened. She had asked for an expression of God's grace, three wounds, which she identified as contrition, compassion and a longing for God. In May 1373 she got everything she had requested.[5]

Julian is a historical role model who ministered out of a sense of spiritual authority and out of an amazing sense of being. In a day when women had few opportunities in positions of leadership, Julian set the pace as a role model who expressed her unique voice unaffected by the dictates of a special office. Weber makes a worthy comment on the pacesetting way in which Julian and other women monastics were influential role models.

> Female monastics (such as Julian) organized and ran their own communities, where they prayed, worked, studied and taught; and female recluses could influence people outside their anchorage walls. Some women thus became accomplished biblical scholars and theologians, which never would have happened had they pursued more usual lifestyles. Others were renowned for their spirituality and became sought-after advisors to bishops and popes and spiritual directors for both men and women.... Such women made up in piety and spiritual power what they lacked in official standing or institutional clout.[6]

A Woman's Voice in a Man's World

Women monastics in the Middle Ages had an enormous effect on the church. In what is sometimes mistakenly understood as a man's world, women monastics like Julian were sought out by many others, men and women alike, for spiritual insight and guidance. From the twelfth century onward women's voices were heard in the teaching roles of such women as Hildegard of Bingen, known as a prophet, Mechtild of Magdeburg, Mechtild of Hackeborn, Catherine of Genoa, Catherine of Siena and Teresa of Ávila.

Julian's notable work *Revelations of Divine Love* has influenced the church's understanding of the intimacy of God's love. Although she was a mystic, contemplative and anchorite, Julian's writing addresses intellectual themes of theology such as creation, incarnation, grace, sin, the church, and the death and resurrection of Jesus. She obviously was well educated, or at least well read in the classical spiritual writings of the Western church, as were many of the other women listed above. Both Catherine of Siena and Bridget of Sweden were involved in political life, Teresa of Ávila wrote on constitutional law, and Juliana of Liege was influential in liturgical development. Such women were not always granted voice in a man's world, but they were given voice through intimacy with God.

Julian illustrates the spirituality of attention to the presence of God in everything in several notable statements:

> And in this he showed me something small, no bigger than a hazelnut, lying in the palm of my hand, and I perceived that it was as round as any ball. I looked at it and thought: What can this be? And I was given this general answer: It is everything which is made. I was amazed that it could last, for I thought that it was so little that it could suddenly fall into nothing. And I was answered in my understanding: It lasts and always will, because God loves it; and thus everything has being through the love of God.[7]

Later she said, "By this vision I saw that he is present in all things."[8]

> The place which Jesus takes in our soul he will nevermore vacate, for in us is his home of homes, and it is the greatest delight for him to dwell there. This was a delectable and a restful sight, for it is so in truth forevermore; and to contemplate this while we are here is most pleasing to God, and very great profit to us. And the soul who thus contemplates is made like to him who is contemplated, and united to him in rest and peace. And it was a singular joy and bliss to me that I saw him sit, for the contemplation of this sitting revealed to me the certainty that he will dwell in us forever; and I knew truly that it was he who had revealed everything to me before.[9]

> God wants us to pay attention to his words, and always to be strong in our certainty, in well-being and in woe, for he loves us and delights in us, and so he wishes us to love him and delight in him and trust greatly in him, all will be well.[10]

Julian of Norwich can serve as a striking example of the devout pursuit of an intimate relationship with God and of how a mentor can assist others to achieve that same depth of relationship. She understood that her visions were given not as a special spiritual privilege for her as one of the monastic elite but rather as a blessed teaching for all. She didn't believe herself to have an experience that was different from those God desired to give everyone. Her experience of God, she said, was not given to her because of some worthiness or uniqueness. God has this same love for all.

Everything that I say about me I mean to apply to all my fellow Christians, for I am taught that is what the Lord intends in this spiritual revelation. . . . I am not good because of the revelations, but only if I love God better; and inasmuch as you love God better, it is more to you than to me. I do not say this to those who are wise, because they know it well. But I say it to you who are simple, to give you comfort and strength; for we are all one in love, for truly it was not revealed to me that God loves me better than the humblest soul who is in a state of grace.[11]

It is God's will that we receive three things from him as gifts as we seek. The first is that we seek willingly and diligently without sloth, as that may be with his grace, joyfully and happily, without unreasonable depression and useless sorrow. The second is that we wait for him steadfastly, out of love for him, without grumbling and contending against him, to the end of our lives, for that will last only for a time. The third is that we have great trust in him, out of complete and true faith, for it is his will that we know that he will appear, suddenly and blessedly, to all his lovers.[12]

Her voice was given expression as she wrote with skill and profound competence in her use of the Latin Vulgate text of the Bible. To read her *Revelations of Divine Love* is an experience of mysticism and theology, fused by a skillful writer's hand. It begins simply as a journal of her experience with God:

Here is a vision shown by the goodness of God to a devout woman, and her name is Julian, who is a recluse at Norwich and still alive, A.D. 1413, in which vision are very many words of comfort, greatly moving for all those who desire to be Christ's lovers.[13]

She tells of her own devotional life and its patterns of prayer, contemplation and careful reflection on Scripture. Her descriptions are graphic and visually haunting, especially as she describes the bleeding body of Christ, glorified and exalted, yet still on his cross. It does not remain a simple description or even a profound description of her personal experience; instead she carefully and reflectively weaves the fundamentals of Christian theology into her writing. She is especially interested to ponder the role of the Trinity, human sinfulness and redemption. Her work makes reference to the thinking of the Scholastic theologian Thomas Aquinas, and the writings of Geoffrey Chaucer are evident in her work.

She is a wonderfully evangelical teacher, for her primary concern is with God, the human family and reconciliation between God and fallen sinful humankind. Everything is filtered through the person of Christ the Servant, the incarnate one whose death and resurrection bring redemption and reconciliation. She thinks of God in trinitarian categories of Father, Son and Holy Spirit but contributes her own voice in her insistence that God has a motherly image. She reminds us of Isaiah 66:13, which says that God will comfort Israel "as a mother comforts her child." She quotes Jesus, who used maternal language to describe God as a mother hen intent on gathering her young under her wings. Her desire is not to make God into an exclusively feminine image but rather to evoke a more fully developed theology of the Trinity. God gives us life and nourishes life; God makes us grow through mercy and tenderness. The motherhood of God, for Julian, is not antithetical to the fatherhood of God but a complement or completion of theological truth.

> And so I saw that God rejoices that he is our Father, and God rejoices that he is our Mother, and God rejoices that he is our true spouse and that our soul is his beloved wife. And Christ rejoices that he is our brother, and Jesus rejoices that he is our savior.[14]

She closes her book with a remarkable doxology with hope that it fall into the hands only of those who "wish to be his faithful lovers." They are true, she says, true to the Holy Church and true to the teachings of Scripture and true to the heart of Jesus, "our true love and light and truth who will show this to all pure souls who meekly and perseveringly ask this wisdom from him."[15] She dared to believe that it came from Jesus "for a safe guide and conduct for you and us to everlasting bliss."[16] Her eyes were opened, and she gave voice to her vision. In one of the most amazing texts of the Middle Ages, Julian shows us the way to intimacy with God and true identity as the beloved of God. Her voice speaks with theological precision and devotional passion. Since almost nothing is known about her life, we cannot tell in what other ways she may have used her window to the world for the sake of the kingdom. That she was teacher, theologian and mentor to many is tribute enough.

Julian serves as a wonderful example of the goal for the work of spiritual mentoring—to empower the mentoree to discover the voice God has placed within. Likewise, in Spain a century later, Teresa's intimate friendship with God led her to a strengthened voice that found its power in the vocabulary of reform. J. Mary Luti says, "As Teresa's friendship with God matured, her world began to look and feel different. She noticed things askew, and began to have a great deal to say about the discrepancies that kept cropping up between her experience of God and what others were claiming to be God's nature and plan."[17]

Teresa of Ávila set out to establish a convent limited to thirteen women and created a furor across Spain! She not only survived the outrage against her little house of Saint Joseph, but she developed seventeen others before her death. Her voice was heard most eloquently in the hundreds of letters she wrote to everyone in power: the king, the pope, merchants, bishops, religious superiors, noblemen and women, and family and friends. At one point she spoke scornfully about those who opposed her reforms as she described their "astonish[ment] at such boldness that a *useless little woman* should found a monastery against their will."[18]

Teresa had practical insights into the life of spirituality. She warned often against settling for the delights of rapturous and mystical visions when perfection lies in conformity to the will of God.[19] Always she sought to merge the life of prayer and the life of obedience as the pathway to God. Her mentoree John of the Cross said, "In the evening they will examine thee in love."[20] Teresa concluded that "the important thing is not to think much, but to love much: do, then, whatever arouses you to love."[21]

J. Mary Luti describes the ultimate source of Teresa's reforming courage and zeal:

> Prayer was, for her, the very source and instrument of courage, daring, and desire. Unless one prayed, that is, cultivated a deep and lasting friendship with God, one could not know and savor the substantial realities upon which authentic courage had to be constructed. In and through prayer, self-knowledge and knowledge of God issued in liberating contempt for the world's values and fearlessness in the face of its ensnaring deceptions— praise, blame, honor, reputation, wealth, status, prideful learning, and the rest. Prayer made the soul bold beyond imagining: the saints' heroic achievements, their near-foolhardy and crazy deeds were explicable for

Teresa only because those women and men were persons enveloped in God through prayer.[22]

In light of Teresa's devotion to God and her commitment to living her life as a reflection of God's will, we remind you again of the ultimate questions in the life of the mentoree: Who is God? Who am I? What does God want to do for his kingdom purposes through my unique voice? The following questions may help you focus on your progress in your goals for spiritual mentoring:

☐ What voice do you discern God has given you?

☐ What is your own unique and particular place of ministry in your world?

☐ Who in your world helps you find boldness and courage to release your God-given voice?

☐ Who discourages the expression of your voice?

☐ What institutions, issues, groups or individuals need to hear your voice, alone or in concert with others?

☐ As a result of weeks or months of mentoring, what do you now believe God intends for your voice, your life?

In the Atrium

We were sitting in the atrium on Grand Avenue outside Starbucks. It's a busy urban neighborhood. A tree overhead, a pot of steaming hot coffee on the table and a book to bring to a conclusion. We sat and wrestled with chapters, sections to include and others to delete. All of the historic mentors have had their say. We know their stories and some of their contributions to the work of spirituality mentoring.

In our imaginations we looked up to see our seven friends from the pages of history walk in and take their places at our table. They were all there: Augustine from North Africa, Aelred from Rivaulx in England, John of the Cross and Teresa of Ávila from Spain along with Ignatius of Loyola, Jeanne Guyon of France and Julian of Norwich in England. "What are you working on today?" they inquired. "We're asking the question, How will we know that the mentors have grown? Now that we've done all the work of attraction, creating trust and intimacy, developing a relationship with disciplines and exercises for growth, how will we know the growth is there in the lives of our mentorees?" And we asked our seven friends to tell us. This is what they said.

Augustine (who else?) began the conversation. "If your mentoree has drawn closer to the heart of God, then you can say they have been mentored well. Insight into divine truth is important, but only if they have made progress in their relationship with God and in their identity as the beloved of God, and have taken steps of active kingdom responsibility in the world." He said, "To such then whom Thou commandest me to serve will I discover, not what I have been but what I now am and yet what I am."[23]

Julian was quick to agree. "The passing life that we lead here, in our sensuality, is not aware of what our true self is, except in faith. When we come to know and see truly and clearly what our self is, then we shall, truly and clearly see and know our Lord God in fullness of joy. And therefore it needs must be that the nearer we are to our bliss, the more we shall long for it, and that both by nature and by grace. . . . And therefore it properly belongeth to us, both by nature and by grace to long and desire, with all our might, to know our self. For in this fullness of knowledge we shall truly and clearly know our God, in fullness of endless joy."[24]

Who is God? Intimacy with God was the starting place for our conversation and serves well as the starting place for assessing the empowerment of mentorees. In what ways have they grown closer in intimacy with God?

Ignatius took us further by pointing out that on our spiritual journey we develop a knowledge of our darkness as well as an understanding of the best in us. "During these Spiritual Exercises one reaches a deeper understanding of the reality and malice of one's sins than when one is not so concentrated on interior concerns."[25] Self-knowledge, he added, is not only for our own self-awareness, but for service. One's ultimate identity is found as one learns of Christ and what it means to give oneself away for the glory of God, in service to God. "Here it will be to ask for interior knowledge of all the great good I have received, in order that, stirred to profound gratitude, I may become able to love and serve his Divine Majesty in all things."[26]

Jeanne Guyon spoke up, saying, "In fact, we are discussing the very thing that caused the early church to lose its life and beauty. It was the loss of a deep, inner, spiritual relationship to Christ. Counterwise, the church could soon be restored if this inner relationship were recovered!"[27]

The quiet Teresa watched with interest and said serenely, "Yet this Lord desires intensely that we love Him and seek His company, so much so that from time to time He calls us to draw near Him. And His voice is so sweet the poor soul dissolves at not doing immediately what He commands."[28] "In my opinion, we shall never completely know ourselves if we don't strive to know God. By gazing at His grandeur, we get in touch with our own lowliness; by looking at His purity, we shall see our own filth, by pondering His humility, we shall see how far we are from being humble."[29]

Jeanne Guyon asked to speak, saying, "When you deal with externals, what you are really doing is driving your soul farther outward from your spirit. The more your spirit is focused on these outward things, the farther it is removed from its center and from its resting place! The result of this type of self-denial is the opposite of what you sought. Unfortunately this is what always happens to a believer when his life is lived out on the surface."[30]

"What then is required of you?" she mused. "All you need to do is remain steadfast in giving your utmost attention to God. He will do all things perfectly. The truth is, not everyone is capable of severe outward self-denial but everyone is capable of turning within and abandoning himself wholly to God."[31]

Who am I? Ultimate identity as the beloved of God was the second answer to which they all pointed. Self-knowledge is ultimately God knowledge. Intimacy with God creates a deepened knowledge of our own identity as God's beloved. We die to self and discover a new depth of self as we learn to see ourselves through the accepting eyes of God's love.

Teresa was emphatic: she wanted us to know that God delights in our very souls. For Teresa, one's identity is first defined by God, given by God and shaped by God and secondarily shaped through relationships and vocation. John of the Cross reminded us that we would have to leave the security of the familiar, known self in order to discover the true self deep within our souls. Intimacy with God leads to the empowerment of knowing one's ultimate identity as the beloved of God.

On one thing they all seemed to agree with Guyon, that life is for joy. "Our ultimate purpose is to enjoy God . . . in this life. To enjoy God! This is the very purpose for which we were created. . . . To serve God is to reign."[32] Julian smiled: "The seeking with faith, hope and charity pleaseth our Lord; the finding pleaseth the soul and fulfilleth it with joy."[33] She couldn't stop: "Our Lord is full of mirth and gladness because of our prayer. For, with His grace, it maketh us like to Him in condition, as we are in kind; and such is his blessed will."[34] Listen again, she said, "for it is His liking to reign in our understanding blissfully, and to sit in our soul restfully, and to dwell in our soul endlessly, working us all into Him. In which working He willeth that we be His helpers, giving to Him all our mind; learning His laws, keeping His counsels, desiring that all be done that He doeth, truly trusting in Him. For verily I saw that our substance is in God."[35]

John, quietly listening across the table, chimed in, "God communicates the mystery of the Trinity to this sinner in such a way that if His Majesty did not strengthen my weakness by a special help, it would be impossible for me to live."[36] Ignatius, always alert to find ways to teach the rest, said, "Human beings are created to praise, reverence and serve God our Lord and by means of this to save their soul."[37]

We interrupted with our own questions: "Your words make it sound as if the life of mature believers is passive or caught up in mystical acts of worship and praise. Is that the goal of our spiritual formation, to experience a mystical union with Christ?"

Ignatius was quick to reply, "Love ought to manifest itself more by deeds than by words."[38] During times of contemplation, he asked mentorees to wonder, "What have I done for Christ? What am I doing for Christ? What ought I do for Christ?"[39] He made his point even more specifically: "Love consists in a mutual sharing of goods for example, the lover gives and shares with the beloved what he possesses, or something of that which he has or is able to give; and vice versa, the beloved shares with the lover."[40]

Teresa, the doctor of mystical union with Christ, looked at the others in nodding agreement. "Teresa makes a final plea that love be not idle. One so intimate with His Majesty must walk with special care and attentiveness in the exercise of virtue and with particular emphasis on love of neighbor, humility (the desire to be considered the least) and the faithful performance of ordinary tasks."[41] The result of union with Jesus will be good works. "Thus even though our works are small they will have the value our love for Him would have merited had they been great."[42] It was clearly her conviction that the enhancement of one's intimate relationship with God would result in a life of Spirit-guided, Spirit-empowered, Spirit-led service to others.

Ignatius was excited: "Consider how the Lord of all the world chooses so many persons, apostles, disciples, and the like. He sends them throughout the whole world, to spread his doctrine among people of every state and condition."[43]

Aelred said, "By whatever means are in one's power, one ought to raise the weak, support the infirm, console the afflicted, restrain the wrathful. Furthermore, one ought so to respect the eye of a friend as to dare to do nothing which is dishonorable or dare to say nothing which is unbecoming."[44]

Teresa was pensive. "Let us understand, my daughters, that true perfection consists in love of God and neighbor; the more perfectly we keep these two commandments the more perfect we will be."[45]

What am I to do with my life? Unique voice, for our friends, became a metaphor for kingdom responsibility. Because I have walked in intimacy with God and know myself to be the beloved of God, I discover an empowerment of a voice, a vocation, a calling, a life to be lived and given to others for the sake of the kingdom.

Julian had the last word as she summarized the three empowerments to which we were shown: intimacy with God, identity as the beloved of God, discovery of a unique voice for kingdom service. "When we give our minds, by the working of mercy and grace, to love and meekness, we are made all fair and clean.... Here we may see that He is Himself this Charity; and He doeth to us as He teacheth us to do to others. For He willeth that we be like Him in wholeness of endless love to ourselves to our even-Christians.... He wills that we should hate the sin itself, and endlessly the soul of the sinner as God loveth it; then we would hate sin as God hateth it, and love the soul as God loveth it."[46]

We were about to leave when Teresa burst into a song:

My God,
let me sing of your mercies
for all eternity,
since it has been your pleasure
so generously to lavish them upon me
that those who see them are amazed,
and I myself wonder at them;
then I burst into songs of praise to you.[47]

She concluded with another paean to God.

O God, your goodness is infinite:
I see clearly who you are

and who I am.
O joy of angels,
when I contemplate
that vast difference between us
I long to be wholly consumed
with love for you. . . .
Life of all lives,
you do not condemn those who trust in you
and want you as a friend:
thus you sustain the life of the body
and give it its health,
along with the life of the soul.[48]

Further Reflection for the Mentor

1. What do you notice of God in fresh ways through the emerging voice of your mentoree?

2. In what ways are you actively seeking to free the voice of your mentoree to sing his or her own music with God-given gifts?

3. What challenges have you made to your mentoree to seek ways to serve, to love, to give and to proclaim the gospel in the larger public square?

4. How do you model a life of engagement rather than disengagement, from the pain of the world?

Further Reflection for the Mentoree

1. In what ways are you beginning to hear your own voice?

2. In which direction(s) do the windows of your soul open? In which direction does the imagery from Julian move you—inwardly or outwardly?

3. How does your life reflect an intimate relationship with God?

4. Where do you gain your sense of identity?

5. What do you perceive to be your unique voice for kingdom service?

Appendix One

Clinton's Mentoring Types

J. Robert Clinton has identified nine types of mentoring relationships, which can be divided into three categories.

Active Mentoring Relationships
   1. Discipler (enabler in the basics of following Christ)
☐ Prayer: speaking and listening
☐ Word: intake and application
☐ Community: acceptance and involvement
☐ Ministry: experiencing and discovering
☐ Doctrines: guiding theological perspectives
   2. Spiritual guide (provides accountability, direction and insight for decision making)
☐ Deepens the believer's spiritual maturity level
☐ Deals with inner-growth issues
☐ Appraises a person's spirituality
☐ Seeks to create internal spiritual motivation
☐ Belongs to the work of the Holy Spirit
☐ Focuses primarily on the enhancement of intimacy with God
☐ Is essential to character formation
☐ Encourages the ongoing process through the journey of faith
☐ Provides perspective for a more effective life of service
   3. Coach (provides motivation, skills and application needed to meet a task)
☐ Guides a skill-focused relationship
☐ Provides motivation
☐ Imparts skills
☐ Shares specific areas of expertise

☐ Breaks desired skills into "bite-sized" pieces
☐ Can instill gentle yet firm discipline
☐ Focuses on obedience and responsibility

The active mentoring relationships require regular interaction and intentionality while working through all five mentoring movements enumerated in the Anderson/Reese Model of Spiritual Mentoring.

Occasional Mentoring Relationships

4. Counselor (offers timely advice on viewing self, others, circumstances and ministry)
☐ Uses spiritual gift of exhortation
☐ Happens nonprofessionally or informally
☐ Provides timely advice and perspective for emerging leaders
☐ Provides stimulus toward potential

5. Teacher (knowledge and understanding of a particular subject)
☐ Format may be formal or informal
☐ Empowerment increases with informality
☐ Provides motivation toward learning
☐ Focuses on integration of theory and practice
☐ Differentiates between styles of learning

6. Sponsor (provides career guidance and development within an organization)
☐ Influences others
☐ Advocates for mentoree within context of an organization
☐ Networks resources to facilitate development
☐ Provides assistance for people to reach potential
☐ Provides career guidance and protection
☐ Can accelerate leadership formation
☐ Matches developmental needs of the individual and organization

Occasional mentoring consists primarily of attraction, responsiveness and empowerment while relationship and accountability are not necessarily present (Clinton 1991:6.1).

Passive Mentoring Relationships

7. Contemporary model (a living, personal model who inspires emulation)
☐ A means for acquiring values and skills

☐ A means to vicarious learning
☐ A self-directed imitation model of mentoring
☐ A means for discovering sense of destiny
    8. Historical model (a past life that teaches dynamic principles)
☐ Examples of those who "finished well"
☐ A necessity for movement toward focused leadership
☐ Timely source of motivation
☐ A means to vicarious learning of skills and values
    9. Divine contact (a timely and divine intervention of guidance or discernment)
☐ Critical encounter that dramatically shapes a life
☐ Timely networking for resources and opportunities
☐ Source of perspective, clarification, confirmation and motivation
☐ Strategic voice during times of crisis or boundary
    The passive category provides a rich resource of mentoring without the necessity of a mentoring relationship (Clinton 1991:2.23).

Appendix Two

Contemporary Definitions of Spiritual Mentoring

Author	Definition of Spiritual Mentoring	Unique Perspectives
William A. Barry and William J. Connolly	"We define Christian spiritual direction, then, as help given by one Christian to another which enables that person to pay attention to God's personal communication to him or her, to respond to this personally communicating God, to grow in intimacy with God, and to live out the consequences of the relationship" (1983:8).	☐ Mentor helps mentoree "listen" to what God desires to say to the mentoree. ☐ Mentoree responds to God. ☐ Mentoree grows in intimacy with God. ☐ Mentoree is responsible to live out directives from enhanced growth.
Marie Coombs and Francis Nemeck	"Spiritual direction then is concerned with discerning the spiritualizing influence of God within the directee as manifested in and through his/her thoughts, feelings, desires, aspirations, activities and relationships. . . . The director and the directee listening together to God discern his influence within the directee as well as the spiritualizing direction he indicates" (1984:66).	☐ Mentor and mentoree discern God's influence in the life of the mentoree ☐ Approach affects various dimensions of the mentoree's being. ☐ Mentor and mentoree "listen" to God's action together. ☐ God directs mentoree in spirituality.

Author	Definition of Spiritual Mentoring	Unique Perspectives
Tilden Edwards	"Being a spiritual friend is being the physician of a wounded soul. And what does a physician do when someone comes with a bleeding wound? Three things: He or she cleanses the wound, aligns the sundered parts, and gives rest. That's all. The physician does not heal. He or she provides an environment for the dominant natural process of healing to take its course. The physician really is midwife rather than healer" (1980:125).	☐ Intimacy of mentoring relationship facilitates growth. ☐ Mentor provides atmosphere for cleansing to take place. ☐ Mentor creates an awareness of interior life. ☐ Mentor provides suggestions to enhance God's action in the life of the mentoree. ☐ God is the one who heals.
Richard J. Foster	"What is the purpose of a spiritual director? . . . His direction is simply and clearly to lead us to our real director. He is the means of God to open the path to the inward teaching of the Holy Spirit" (1988:185).	☐ Process leads mentoree to experience God. ☐ Mentor provides atmosphere to discover inner movement of the Holy Spirit.
Margaret Guenther	Spiritual direction is "recognizing God's amazing work in us and among us in the ordinariness of human existence. . . . It holds up the demands of absolute responsibility and the promise of absolute forgiveness" (1992:xiii).	☐ Method recognizes God's inner work in the life of the mentoree. ☐ Process provides realization of forgiveness. ☐ Progress calls for responsibility.
Alan W. Jones	"The object of spiritual direction is to help us keep in touch with Jesus as the key to true companionship. . . . Spiritual direction seeks to guide us deeper into the double mystery of God and of ourselves by means of companionship" (1982:47).	☐ Method encourages *intimacy with God *deeper issues of spirituality *understanding of one's self *intimacy in a mentoring relationship

Author	Definition of Spiritual Mentoring	Unique Perspectives
Jean Laplace	"Direction can be defined as the help that one man gives another to enable him to become himself in his faith" (1988:26).	☐ Direction accomplished in context of a mentoring relationship. ☐ Mentor encourages self-awareness of mentoree. ☐ Mentor creates atmosphere for responsible spiritual growth of the mentoree.
Kenneth Leech	"It is an art which includes helping to discern the movements of the Holy Spirit in our life, assisting in the difficult task of obedience to these movements, and offering support in the crucial life decisions that our faithfulness requires" (summary of Leech's thoughts on spiritual direction, by Henri Nouwen 1977:vi).	☐ Spiritual direction *provides discernment of God's action *accountability and motivation *encouragement *intimate relationship that allows the discovery of intimacy with God
Thomas Merton	"The whole purpose of spiritual direction is to penetrate beneath the surface of a man's life, to get behind the facade of conventional gestures and attitudes which he presents to the world, and to bring out his inner spiritual freedom, his inmost truth, which is what we call the likeness of Christ in his soul" (1960:16).	☐ Spiritual direction *fosters authenticity in mentoree *reveals deeper dimensions of spirituality *impacts actions and attitudes *facilitates discovery of spiritual identity *requires forthrightness and discernment of mentor
Eugene Peterson	"This is the pastoral work that is historically termed the cure of souls. ... The cure of souls, then, is the Scripture-directed, prayer-shaped care that is devoted to persons singly or in groups, to	☐ Spiritual direction *is biblically based *is shaped in an attitude of prayer *is done individually or in groups

Author	Definition of Spiritual Mentoring	Unique Perspectives
Eugene Peterson (continued)	concentrate on the essential.... The cure of the souls is cultivated awareness that God has already seized the initiative. ... God has been working diligently, redemptively, and strategically before I appeared on the scene, before I was aware there was something here for me to do" (1989:66-69).	*recognizes the already present work of God in the mentoree *seeks to listen to what God is already doing in the life of the mentoree *requires discernment and Spirit sensitivity in the mentor

Appendix Three

Historical Time Line of the Christian Classics

Augustine 354-430	Aelred of Rievaulx 1110-1167	Julian of Norwich 1342-1416	Ignatius of Loyola 1491-1556	Teresa of of Ávila 1515-1582	John of the Cross 1542-1591	Jeanne Guyon 1648-1717

Classic Christian Author	Perspective on Spiritual Mentoring	Focus
Augustine (354-430)	"My guardian is sufficient for me.... To such then whom Thou commandest me to serve will I discover not what I have been, but what I now am and what I yet am. *But neither do I judge myself.* Thus therefore, I would be heard" (Weber 1994:130).	Augustine's contribution to this volume is seen in chapter three, "The Art of Beginning Well: Attraction." Augustine's insight sets the tone as we seek to challenge the mentor to follow the wisdom of this saint: "Attract them by your way of life."
Aelred of Rievaulx (1110-1167)	"Here we are. You and I, and I hope a third is also present— Christ Himself. Since no one else is here to disturb us, open your heart and let me hear what you have to say" (Laker 1977:51).	We discuss this twelfth-century exemplar of spiritual friendship in chapter four, "Developing Trust and Intimacy: Relationship." Aelred's perspectives are presented in terms of the need to provide a hospitable space for the spiritual mentoring relationship.

Classic Christian Author	Perspective on Spiritual Mentoring	Focus
Julian of Norwich (1342-1416)	"I say fully truly that all our endless friendship, our station, our life and our being is in God" (Weber 1994:386).	Julian of Norwich is discussed in chapter seven, "The Goal of Spiritual Mentoring: Empowerment," a fitting chapter for this resilient woman who in the midst of darkness pointed her mentorees toward the recognition of their unique voices for kingdom service.
Ignatius of Loyola (1491-1556)	"For just as taking a walk, traveling on foot, and running are physical exercises, so is the name of spiritual exercises given to any means of preparing and disposing our soul to rid itself of all its disordered affections and then, after their removal, of seeking and finding God's will in the ordering of our life for the salvation of our soul. (Ganss 1991:121)	Attention is given to Ignatius of Loyola in chapter six, "Exercises of Grace: Accountability." His exercises provide timeless direction to assist the mentor in the role of keeping the mentoree accountable during the spiritual mentoring relationship.
Teresa of Ávila (1515-1582)	"It is a wonderful thing for a person to talk to those who speak about this interior castle, to draw near not only to those seen to be in these rooms where he is, but to those known to have entered the one closer to the center. Conversations with these latter will be a great help to him, and he can converse so much with them that they will bring him to where they are" (Kavanaugh and Rodriquez 1980:300).	Chapter five, "The Spirit of Teachability: Responsiveness," is the primary focus for the insights from Teresa. The prayer movement of the "seven rooms" or "dwelling places" directs the mentor in guiding the mentoree through the various stages of prayer in order to foster a greater responsiveness to the inner working of the Spirit.

Classic Christian Author	Perspective on Spiritual Mentoring	Focus
John of the Cross (1542-1591)	"These directors should reflect that they themselves are not the chief agent, guide, and mover of souls in this matter, but that the principle guide is the Holy Spirit, Who is never neglectful of souls, and that they are instruments for directing them to perfection through faith and the law of God, according to the spirit of God gives each one. (Kavanaugh and Rodriguez 1979:627).	John of the Cross is also given expression in chapter five. His life reflects the essence of this chapter on "responsiveness" as he submitted himself to the mentoring of Teresa of Ávila. John's "dark night of the soul" movement of prayer is also used as a suggested model in order to create within the mentoree a responsiveness to the working of the Spirit.
Jeanne Guyon (1648-1717)	"It has been the habit of man throughout the ages to heal people by applying some remedy to the outward body when, in fact, the disease is deep inside. Why do converts remain basically unchanged despite so much effort? It is because those over them have dealt only with the outward matters of their lives. There is a better way: Go straight to the heart! . . . Teach a believer to seek God within his own heart" (G. Edwards 1975:121).	Madame Jeanne Guyon was sought out by political and church leaders for her ability to create a safe space where the spiritual seeker could learn to discern God's direction. For that reason she deserves a rightful place alongside Aelred of Rievaulx in chapter four, "Developing Trust and Intimacy: Relationship."

Appendix Four

Developing a
Personal Time Line

These suggestions are adapted from Clinton's "Ministry Time-line." Detailed analysis of an emerging leader's progression along the ministry timeline can be seen in J. Robert Clinton, *Leadership Emergence Theory* (Altadena, Calif.: Barnabas, 1989). The purpose of this exercise is to allow an emerging leader to analyze his or her progression of development. A critical incident is defined as a key relationship, experience or circumstance that has proven to be a shaping incident in personal development.

PHASE I FOUNDATIONS	PHASE II GROWTH	PHASE III FOCUS	PHASE IV CONVERGENCE

A ⟶ B ⟶ A ⟶ B ⟶ C ⟶ A ⟶ B ⟶ A ⟶ B ⟶ C ⟶

Phase I: Foundations

A. Sovereign Foundations: early shaping of character, personality and values

B. Leadership Transition: first steps in discovering ministry and sense of call

Phase II: Growth

A Provisional: first attempts at full-time vocational assignments

B. Growth: utilization of known giftedness, discovery of role preference and leadership focus

C. Competence: performing ministry in roles that fit giftedness; identity questions emerge

Phase III: Focus

A. Role Transition: moving to compatibility in gifts, role, passion and calling

B. Uniqueness: leading with unique efficiency out of spiritual authority base

Phase IV: Convergence

A. Special Guidance: moving toward a role focusing on legacy

B. Convergence: fulfillment of a sense of destiny

C. Afterglow: fallout of effects of finishing well; spiritual authority

Steps in Building a Personal Time Line

1. Draw a horizontal line, placing birth date at left end and present date on right.

2. Mark the date you began vocational or bivocational ministry.

3. Plot critical incidents between birth date and ministry entry date (phase I).

4. Review in your journal critical incidents during this "foundations" phase

5. Plot critical incidents between ministry entry date and present date.

6. Plot various "seasons" or experiences of ministry in this second phase.

7. Review in your journal critical incidents and ministry times during this phase.

8. Analyze your developmental progression against the time line above.

9. Create a list of the common themes that emerge from your time-line story.

10. Review your time-line themes with a spiritual mentor.

Appendix Five

Recommended Bibliography for Spiritual Mentoring

Aelred of Rievaulx
  1977   *Spiritual Friendship.* Translated by Mary Eugenia Laker. Kalamazoo, Mich.: Cistercian.

Allen, Joseph J.
  1994   *Inner Way: Toward a Rebirth of Eastern Christian Spiritual Direction.* Grand Rapids, Mich.: Eerdmans.

Barry, William A., and
William J. Connolly
  1983   *The Practice of Spiritual Direction.* New York: Seabury.

Biehl, Bob
  1996   *Mentoring: Confidence in Finding a Mentor and Becoming One.* Nashville: Broadman and Holman.

Clinton, J. Robert
  1989   *Leadership Emergence Theory.* Altadena, Calif.: Barnabas.

  1991   *The Mentor Handbook: Detailed Guidelines and Helps for Christian Mentors and Mentorees.* Altadena, Calif.: Barnabas.

Coombs, Marie Theresa,
and Francis Kelly Nemeck
  1984   *The Way of Spiritual Direction.* Collegeville, Minn.: Liturgical.

Edwards, Tilden
  1980   *Spiritual Friend: Reclaiming the Gift of Spiritual Direction.* New York: Paulist.

Engstrom, Ted, and
Norman B. Rohrer
  1989   *The Fine Art of Mentoring.* Brentwood, Tenn.: Wolgemuth and Hyatt.

Fleming, Daniel J., S. J.
1996   *Draw Me Into Your Friendship: The Spiritual Exercises.* St.
             Louis: The Institute of Jesuit Sources.

Foster, Richard J.
1988   *Celebration of Discipline.* 2nd ed. New York: Harper & Row.

1998   *Streams of Living Water: Celebrating the Great Traditions of
             Christian Faith.* San Francisco: Harper

Gratton, Carolyn
1992   *The Art of Spiritual Guidance: A Contemporary Approach to
             Growing in the Spirit.* New York: Crossroad.

Guenther, Margaret
1992   *The Art of Spiritual Direction.* Cambridge, Mass.:
             Cowley.

Guyon, Jeanne
1975   *Experiencing the Depths of Jesus Christ.* Edited by Gene
             Edwards. Beaumont, Tex.: Seed Sowers.

Hart, Archibald
1996   *How to Find the Help You Need.* Grand Rapids, Mich.:
             Zondervan.

Hausherr, Irene
1990   *Spiritual Direction in the Early Christian East.* Kalamazoo,
             Mich.: Cistercian.

Hendricks, Howard, and
Bill Hendricks
1995   *As Iron Sharpens Iron.* Chicago: Moody Press.

Houston, James M.
1983   Introduction to Bernard of Clairvaux, *The Love of God,*
             and Aelred of Rievaulx, *Spiritual Friendship.* Portland,
             Ore.: Multnomah Press.

Ignatius of Loyola
1991   *The Spiritual Exercises and Selected Works.* Edited by
             George E. Ganss. New York: Paulist.

John of the Cross
1979   *The Collected Works.* Translated by Kieran Kavanaugh and
             Otilio Rodriguez. Washington, D.C.: Institute of
             Carmelite Studies, 1979.

Johnson, Ben Campbell
1991   *Speaking of God: Evangelism as Initial Spiritual Guidance.*
             Louisville, Ky.: Westminster John Knox.

Jones, Alan W.
1982   *Exploring Spiritual Direction.* New York: Seabury.

Jones, Cheslyn, Geoffrey
Wainwright and Edward
Yarnold, eds.

1985   *The Study of Spirituality.* New York: Oxford University Press.

Kelsey, Morton T.

1995   *Companions on the Inner Way.* New York: Crossroad.

Kelly, Thomas R.

1969   *A Testament of Devotion.* San Franciso: Harper.

Laplace, Jean

1988   *Preparing for Spiritual Direction.* 3rd ed. Chicago: Franciscan Herald.

Leech, Kenneth

1977   *Soul Friend: The Practice of Christian Spirituality.* San Francisco: Harper & Row.

Merton, Thomas

1960   *Spiritual Direction and Meditation.* Collegeville, Minn.: Liturgical.

Nouwen, Henri J. M.

1997   *Adam: God's Beloved.* Maryknoll, N.Y.: Orbis, 1997.

Peterson, Eugene H.

1989   *The Contemplative Pastor: Returning to the Art of Spiritual Direction.* Dallas: Word.

Stanley, Paul, and
J. Robert Clinton

1992   *Connecting: The Mentoring Relationships You Need to Succeed in Life.* Colorado Springs: NavPress.

Teresa of Ávila

1976-1985   The Collected Works. 3 vols. Translated by Kieran Kavanaugh and Otilio Rodriguez. Washington, D.C.: Institute of Carmelite Studies.

1995   *Perfect Love: The Meditations, Prayers and Writings of Teresa of Ávila.* Edited by Trace Murphy. New York: Doubleday, 1995.

Weber, Timothy P., ed.

1994   *The Treasury of Christian Spiritual Classics.* Nashville Thomas Nelson.

Willard, Dallas

1998   *The Divine Conspiracy: Rediscovering Our Hidden Life in God.* San Francisco: HarperSanFrancisco.

Notes

Chapter 1: An Imitative Faith

[1] Thomas à Kempis, *The Imitation of Christ* (Grand Rapids, Mich.: Zondervan, 1967), p. 1.

[2] George Lane, *Christian Spirituality: An Historical Sketch* (Chicago: Loyola University Press, 1984), p. v.

[3] Elizabeth A. Dreyer, *Earth Crammed with Heaven* (New York: Paulist, 1994), p. 34.

[4] Tilden Edwards, *Spiritual Friendship: Reclaiming the Gift of Spiritual Direction* (New York: Paulist, 1980), p. 35.

[5] "God's Grandeur," in *Poems and Prose of Gerard Manley Hopkins*, ed. W. H. Gardner (Baltimore: Penguin, 1963), p. 27.

[6] Walter Brueggemann, *The Creative Word* (Philadelphia: Fortress, 1982), p. 1.

[7] Kenneth Leech, *Soul Friend: An Invitation to Spiritual Direction* (San Francisco: Harper, 1977), p. 41.

[8] Ibid.

[9] Ibid., p. 68.

[10] Hopkins, "God's Grandeur."

[11] W. B. Yeats, *The Variorum Edition of the Poems of W. B. Yeats,* ed. Peter Allt and Russel K. Alspach (New York: Macmillan, 1977), p. 553.

[12] Barbara Brown Taylor, *The Preaching Life* (Boston: Cowley, 1993), p. 15.

Chapter 2: Reading Between the Lines

[1] Thomas Merton, *Spiritual Direction and Meditation* (Collegeville, Minn.: Order of St. Benedict Press, 1960), p. 16.

[2] Jeanne Guyon, *Experiencing the Depths of Jesus Christ*, ed. Gene Edwards (Beaumont, Tex.: Seed Sowers, 1975), pp. 143-44.

[3] Ibid., pp. 7-8.

[4] Philip Babcock Gove, ed., *Webster's Third International Dictionary* (Springfield, Mass.: G. & C. Merriam, 1981), p. 1412.

[5] J. Robert Clinton, *The Mentor Handbook* (Altadena, Calif.: Barnabas, 1991).

[6] Eugene Peterson, *The Contemplative Pastor: Returning to the Art of Spiritual Direction* (Carol Stream, Ill.: Christianity Today; Dallas: Word, 1989), p. 119.

[7] Alan Jones, *Passion for Pilgrimage* (San Francisco: Harper, 1989), p. 4.

[8] Ibid., p. 20.

[9] Irenaeus, *Five Books of Saint Irenaeus, Bishop of Lyons, Against Heresies*, ed. John Keble (Oxford: J. Parker, 1872), 4.40.6.

[10] Margaret Guenther, *Holy Listening: The Art of Spiritual Direction* (Cambridge, Mass.: Cowley, 1992), p. xi.

[11] Eugene Peterson, *Under the Unpredictable Plant: An Exploration in Vocational Holiness* (Grand Rapids, Mich.: Eerdmans, 1992), p. 75.

[12] Ibid., p. 16.

[13] Ibid., p. 86.

[14] Merton, *Spiritual Direction*, p. 16.

[15] Peterson, *Contemplative Pastor*, p. 69.

[16] Kenneth Leech, *Soul Friend: An Invitation to Spiritual Direction* (San Francisco: Harper, 1977), p. vi.

[17]Teresa of Ávila, *The Autobiography of St. Teresa of Ávila*, ed. E. Allison Peers (New York: Doubleday/Image, 1960), pp. 41-41.

[18]Phil Cousineau, *The Art of Pilgrimage* (Berkeley, Calif.: Conari, 1998), pp. xxiii-xxiv.

[19]Thomas Groome, *Educating for Life: A Spiritual Vision for Every Teacher and Parent* (Allen, Tex.: Thomas More, 1998), p. 416.

[20]Carolyn Gratton, *The Art of Spiritual Direction* (New York: Crossroad, 1992), pp. 36-37.

[21]Therese of Lisieux, *Story of a Soul: The Autobiography of St. Therese of Lisieux*, trans. John Clarke (Washington, D.C.: Institute of Carmelite Studies, 1975), p. 113.

[22]Cited in A. Aaudreau, *The Degrees of the Spiritual Life* (London: Burns & Oates, 1926), 2:245.

[23]Ignatius of Loyola, *The Spiritual Exercises of Ignatius Loyola*, trans. Anthony Mottola (New York: Image, 1964), p. 15.

[24]Ted Engstrom, *The Fine Art of Mentoring* (Brentwood, Tenn.: Wolgemuth & Hyatt, 1989), p. 15.

[25]Bobb Biehl, *Mentoring* (Nashville: Broadman and Holman, 1996), p. 59.

[26]Peterson, *Contemplative Pastor*, pp. 183, 185.

[27]Ibid., p. 186.

[28]Ibid.

Chapter 3: The Art of Beginning Well

[1]James M. Houston, introduction to Bernard of Clairvaux, *The Love of God*, and Aelred of Rievaulx, *Spiritual Friendship*, ed. James M. Houston (Portland, Ore.: Multnomah Press, 1983), p. xiv.

[2]Ibid., p. xiv.

[3]Marie Theresa Coombs and Francis Kelly Nemeck, *The Way of Spiritual Direction* (Collegeville, Minn.: Liturgical, 1985), p. 48.

[4]From Timothy P. Weber, ed., *The Treasury of Christian Classics* (Nashville: Thomas Nelson, 1994), p. 5.

[5]Augustine, *The Letters of Saint Augustine*, ed. John Leinenweber (Liguori, Mo.: Triumph, 1992), p. 99.

[6]Eugene Peterson, *Leap over a Wall* (San Francisco: HarperCollins, 1997), pp. 3-4.

[7]J. Robert Clinton, *The Mentor Handbook* (Altadena, Calif.: Barnabas, 1991), p. 1 of chapter 7.

[8]Teresa of Ávila *The Book of Life* 9.8. See Teresa of Ávila, *The Collected Works*, trans. Kieran Kavanaugh and Otilio Rodriguez (Washington, D.C.: Institute of Carmelite Studies, 1976), 1:73.

[9]Aelred of Rievaulx, *Spiritual Friendship*, trans. Mary Eugenia Laker (Kalamazoo, Mich.: Cistercian, 1977), pp. 72-73.

[10]Ibid., p. 83.

[11]Ibid., p. 84.

[12]Ibid., pp. 84-85.

Chapter 4: Developing Trust & Intimacy

[1]J. Robert Clinton, *The Mentor Handbook* (Altadena, Calif.: Barnabas, 1991), p. 16 of chapter 2.

[2]Parker Palmer, *To Know As We Are Known: A Spirituality of Education* (San Francisco: Harper & Row, 1983), p. 69.

[3]Ibid., pp. 69-75.

[4]James M. Houston, introduction to Bernard of Clairvaux, *The Love of God*, and Aelred of

Rievaulx, *Spiritual Friendship*, ed. James M. Houston (Portland, Ore.: Multnomah Press, 1983), p. xvi.

[5]Ibid., p. xxviii.

[6]Aelred of Rievaulx, *Spiritual Friendship*, trans. Mary Eugenia Laker (Kalamazoo, Mich.: Cistercian, 1977), p. 71.

[7]Ibid., p. 72.

[8]Ibid.

[9]Ibid., p. 91.

[10]Ibid., p. 93.

[11]Ibid., p.103.

[12]Ibid., p. 105.

[13]Ibid., pp. 112-13.

[14]Ibid., p. 122.

[15]Ibid., p. 131.

[16]Henri J. M. Nouwen, *Ministry and Spirituality* (New York: Continuum, 1996), p. 217.

[17]Ibid., p. 218.

[18]Ibid., p. 219.

[19]Henri J. M. Nouwen, *Adam, God's Beloved* (Maryknoll, N.Y.: Orbis, 1997), pp. 81-82.

[20]Aelred, *Spiritual Friendship*, p. 120.

[21]Eugene Peterson, *Leap over a Wall* (San Francisco: HarperSanFrancisco, 1997), pp. 60-61.

[22]Andrew Greeley, *Andrew Greeley's Chicago* (Chicago: Contemporary, 1989), frontispiece.

[23]Aelred, *Spiritual Friendship*, p. 51.

[24]Teresa of Ávila, *The Collected Works*, trans. and ed. Kieran Kavanaugh and Otilio Rodriguez (Washington, D.C.: Institute of Carmelite Studies, 1985), 3:119-20.

[25]Dallas Willard, *The Spirit of the Disciplines* (San Francisco: HarperSanFrancisco, 1988), p. 31.

[26]Teresa of Ávila, *Perfect Love* (New York: Doubleday/Image, 1995), p. 146.

Chapter 5: The Spirit of Teachability

[1]J. Robert Clinton, *The Mentor Handbook* (Altadena, Calif.: Barnabas, 1991), p. 17 of chapter 2.

[2]Ibid.

[3]Teresa of Ávila *The Book of Life* 9.8. See Teresa of Ávila, *The Collected Works*, trans. Kieran Kavanaugh and Otilio Rodriguez (Washington, D.C.: Institute of Carmelite Studies, 1979), 2:25.

[4]J. Mary Luti, *Teresa of Ávila's Way* (Collegeville, Minn.: Liturgical, 1991), p. 87.

[5]Cheslyn Jones, Geoffrey Wainright and Edward Yarnold, eds., *The Study of Spirituality* (Oxford: Oxford University Press, 1986), p. 365.

[6]John of the Cross, *The Ascent of Mount Carmel*, in *Selected Writings*, ed. Kieran Kavanaugh (New York: Paulist 1987), p. 143

[7]Quoted in Luti, *Teresa of Ávila's Way*, p. 68.

[8]Ibid., p. 69.

[9]Teresa of Ávila, *The Interior Castle*, trans. and ed. E. Alison Peers (New York: Doubleday/Image, 1989), p. 197.

[10]Ibid., p. 162.

[11]Ibid., pp. 14-15.

[12]Ibid., p. 28.

[13]Ibid., p. 76.

[14]Ibid., p. 231

[15]Ibid., p. 229.

[16]*The Collected Works of St. John of the Cross,* trans. Kieran Kavanaugh and Otilio Rodriguez (Washington, D.C.: Institute of Carmelite Studies, 1979), p. 13.

[17]John of the Cross, *Selected Writings,* p. 201.

[18]Ibid.

[19]*Collected Works of St. John of the Cross,* p. 83.

[20]Ibid.

[21]Ibid., p. 164.

[22]Ibid., pp. 77-78.

[23]Ibid., p. 78.

[24]Ibid., p. 164.

[25]Ibid., p. 168.

[26]Ibid., p. 173.

[27]Ibid.

[28]Ibid., p. 174.

[29]Ibid., p. 175

[30]Ibid., pp 175-76.

[31]Ibid., p. 176.

[32]Ibid., p. 177.

[33]Ibid.

[34]Ibid., p. 178.

[35]Ibid., p. 185.

[36]John of the Cross, *Selected Writings,* pp. 78-79.

[37]Ibid., p. 185.

Chapter 6: Exercises of Grace

[1]Thomas R. Kelly, *A Testament of Devotion* (San Francisco: Harper, 1969), p. 93.

[2]J. Robert Clinton, *The Mentor Handbook* (Altadena, Calif.: Barnabas, 1991), p. 18 of chap. 2.

[3]Ignatius of Loyola, *The Spiritual Exercises and Selected Works,* ed. George E. Ganss (New York: Paulist, 1991), p. 10.

[4]Ibid., p. 40.

[5]Ibid., p. 49.

[6]Ibid., pp. 50-51.

[7]Kenneth Leech, *Soul Friend: An Invitation to Spiritual Direction* (San Francisco: Harper, 1977), p. 149.

[8]Ignatius of Loyola, *The Spiritual Exercises of St. Ignatius,* trans. Louis J. Puhl (Chicago: Loyola University Press, 1951), p. 1.

[9]Ibid., p. 78.

[10]Ibid., p. 69.

[11]Ibid., p. 82.

[12]Ibid., p. 90.

[13]Ibid., p. 103.

[14]Ibid., p. 102.

[15]Leech, *Soul Friend,* p. 59.

[16]*The Collected Works of St. John of the Cross,* ed. Kieran Kavanaugh and Otilio Rodriguez (Washington, D.C.: Institute of Carmelite Studies, 1979), p. 63.

[17]Leech, *Soul Friend,* p. 149

[18]Ignatius, *Spiritual Exercises,* ed. Puhl, p. 142.
[19]Ibid
[20]Ibid., p. 143.
[21]Ibid., p. 15.
[22]Leech, *Soul Friend,* p. 149.
[23]Ignatius, *Spiritual Exercises and Selected Works,* ed. Ganss, p. 177.
[24]Ibid., p. 54.
[25]Ibid., p. 25.
[26]Ibid., p. 29.
[27]Ibid.
[28]Ibid., pp. 175-87.
[29]Daniel Taylor, *The Healing Power of Stories* (New York: Doubleday, 1996), p. 21.
[30]Ignatius, *Spiritual Exercises,* ed. Puhl, p. 15.
[31]Joseph Allen, *Inner Way: Toward a Rebirth of Eastern Christian Spiritual Direction* (Grand Rapids, Mich.: Eerdmans, 1994), p. 109.
[32]Thomas Groome, *Educating for Life: A Spiritual Vision for Every Teacher and Parent* (Allen, Tex.: Thomas More, 1998), p. 165.
[33]Wendy Miller, *Learning to Listen* (Nashville, Tenn.: Upper Room, 1993), p. 33.
[34]Julian of Norwich, *Showings,* ed. Edmund Colledge and James Walsh (New York: Paulist, 1978), pp. 152-53.
[35]Dallas Willard, *The Divine Conspiracy: Rediscovering Our Hidden Life in God* (San Francisco: HarperSanFrancisco, 1998), pp. 357-58.
[36]Ibid.
[37]Ibid., p. 361.
[38]Ibid., p. 363.
[39]Jeanne Guyon, *Experiencing the Depths of Jesus Christ,* ed. Gene Edwards (Beaumont, Tex.: Seed Sowers, 1975), pp. 145-46.
[40]Ibid., p. 150.
[41]Ibid., pp. 7-8.
[42]Ibid., pp. 9-10.
[43]James Fowler, *Stages of Faith* (San Francisco: Harper & Row, 1981), p. 30.

Chapter 7: The Goal of Spiritual Mentoring
[1]Gordon Cosby, *Handbook for Mission Groups* (Waco, Tex.: Word, 1975), p. 98.
[2]Annie Dillard, *The Writing Life* (New York: Harper & Row, 1989), p. 68.
[3]Eugene Peterson, *Run with the Horses* (Downers Grove, Ill.: InterVarsity Press, 1983), p. 13.
[4]Julian of Norwich, *Showings,* ed. Edmund Colledge and James Walsh (New York: Paulist, 1978), p. 27
[5]From Timothy P. Weber, ed., *The Treasury of Christian Spiritual Classics* (Nashville: Thomas Nelson, 1994), p. 331.
[6]Ibid., p. 332
[7]Julian, *Showings,* p. 130.
[8]Ibid., p. 137
[9]Ibid., p. 164
[10]Ibid., p. 165
[11]Ibid., p. 191.
[12]Ibid., p. 196

[13]Ibid., p. 125.

[14]Ibid., p. 279.

[15]Ibid., p. 343.

[16]Ibid.

[17]J. Mary Luti, *Teresa of Ávila's Way* (Collegeville, Minn.: Liturgical, 1991), p. 148.

[18]Ibid., p. 76.

[19]Teresa of Ávila, *The Collected Works*, trans. Kieran Kavanaugh and Otilio Rodriguez (Washington, D.C.: Institute of Carmelite Studies, 1985), 3:116-23.

[20]John of the Cross, *The Complete Works*, ed. and trans. E. Allison Peers (London: Burns & Oates, 1953), p. 225.

[21]Teresa of Ávila, *The Interior Castle*, trans. and ed. E. Alison Peers (New York: Doubleday/Image, 1989), p. 76.

[22]Luti, *Teresa of Ávila's Way*, p. 77.

[23]From Weber, *Treasury of Christian Classics*, p. 130.

[24]Ibid., p. 383.

[25]Ignatius of Loyola, *The Spiritual Exercises and Selected Works*, ed. George E. Ganss (New York: Paulist, 1991), p. 135.

[26]Ibid., p. 176.

[27]Jeanne Guyon, *Experiencing the Depths of Jesus Christ*, ed. Gene Edwards (Beaumont, Tex.: Seed Sowers, 1975), pp 118-19.

[28]Teresa of Ávila, *Collected Works*, 2:298.

[29]Ibid., 2:292.

[30]Guyon, *Experiencing the Depths*, p. 50.

[31]Ibid., p. 51.

[32]Ibid., p. 92.

[33]From Weber, *Treasury of Christian Spiritual Classics*, p. 348.

[34]Ibid., p. 378.

[35]Ibid., p. 403.

[36]*The Collected Works of St. John of the Cross*, ed. Kieran Kavanaugh and Otilio Rodriguez (Washington, D.C.: Institute of Carmelite Studies, 1979), p. 31.

[37]Ignatius, *Spiritual Exercises*, ed. Ganss, p. 130.

[38]Ibid., p. 176.

[39]Ibid., p. 138.

[40]Ignatius of Loyola, *The Spiritual Exercises of St. Ignatius*, trans. Louis J. Puhl (Chicago: Loyola University Press, 1951), p. 101.

[41]Teresa of Ávila, *The Collected Works*, trans. Kieran Kavanaugh and Otilio Rodriguez (Washington, D.C.: Institute of Carmelite Studies, 1979), 2:274.

[42]Ibid., 2:278.

[43]Ignatius, *Spiritual Exercises*, ed. Ganss, p. 155.

[44]Aelred of Rievaulx, *Spiritual Friendship*, trans. Mary Eugenia Laker (Kalamazoo, Mich.: Cistercian, 1977), p. 119.

[45]Peers, 1980, pp. 295-96.

[46]From Weber, *Treasury of Christian Classics*, pp. 376-77.

[47]Teresa of Ávila, *Praying with Saint Teresa*, comp. Battistina Capalbo, trans. Paula Clifford (Grand Rapids, Mich.: Eerdmans, 1997), p. 17.

[48]Ibid., p. 37.